LEADING FROM ANYWHERE

LEADING
FROM
ANYWHERE

The Essential Guide
to Managing Remote Teams

David Burkus

Houghton Mifflin Harcourt

BOSTON   NEW YORK

2021

For information about permission to reproduce selections from this book,
write to trade.permissions@hmhco.com or to Permissions,
Houghton Mifflin Harcourt Publishing Company, 3 Park Avenue,
19th Floor, New York, New York 10016.

hmhbooks.com

Library of Congress Cataloging-in-Publication Data is available.
Names: Burkus, David, 1983– author.
Title: Leading from anywhere : the essential guide to managing remote teams
/ David Burkus.
Description: Boston : Houghton Mifflin Harcourt, 2021. |
Includes bibliographical references and index.
Identifiers: LCCN 2020044142 (print) | LCCN 2020044143 (ebook) |
ISBN 9780358533276 (hardcover) | ISBN 9780358573777 |
ISBN 9780358573807 | ISBN 9780358533382 (ebook)
Subjects: LCSH: Virtual reality in management. | Virtual work teams —
Management. | Leadership.
Classification: LCC HD30.2122 .B87 2021 (print) | LCC HD30.2122 (ebook) |
DDC 658.4/022 — dc23
LC record available at https://lccn.loc.gov/2020044142
LC ebook record available at https://lccn.loc.gov/2020044143

Printed in the United States of America
DOC 10 9 8 7 6 5 4 3 2 1

To everyone still working from a cubicle.

Freedom is coming.

Contents

CONTENTS

LEADING FROM ANYWHERE

Introduction

The Rise and Fall — and Rise — of Remote Teams

WHEN HAYDEN BROWN assumed the role of CEO of Upwork on January 1, 2020, she probably never imagined her first year would go quite like it did.

Upwork, a billion-dollar company, was created when Elance and oDesk merged to become the world's largest platform for finding and working with freelance talent. Prior to 2020, most of the company's employees already worked remotely from eight hundred cities around the world. The company had several traditional office locations for employees who weren't ready for remote, but even the office receptionist was a virtual employee who managed multiple front desks from her home office. Under the leadership of Brown's predecessor, Stephane Kasriel, the company that managed the world's largest pool for remote talent had operated as remotely as it could.

Or so they thought.

When a novel coronavirus started spreading rapidly across the globe, Brown and her leadership team found themselves in the same position as many other senior leaders. They had to decide how to respond. They had to figure out how to keep the business operating while also ensuring the safety of all of their stakeholders. But unlike a lot of companies, they didn't decide to send everybody home for a short-term, work-from-home experiment. Instead of a short-term pivot, they saw it as time to commit.

They had done the research. They had been a supporting pillar in the remote-work movement for long enough, but just kept hanging on to their office space. It was time to finalize the inevitable transition to becoming fully remote.

"Building on our 20 years of experience as a remote-work company, we are now permanently embracing a 'remote-first' model. Going forward, working remotely will be the default for everyone," Brown posted on Twitter, ending her post with "The #futureofwork is here."

This is a book about that future. Or, perhaps better stated, this is a book about the past, present, and future of remote teams — and how you can thrive in your role as a leader in that future.

It's difficult to trace the origins of remote teams. On some level, they've always been a reality. The Roman Empire stretched across three continents, but Caesar had to settle for roads and messengers. At the height of its colonialism, it was said the sun never set on the British Empire, but Queen Victoria had to keep it all together using ships and trade routes. Even in the relatively short history of the United States, circuit riders coordinated to preach across the growing country and traveling salesmen went door-to-door even before the automobile to maximize revenue for their companies and themselves.

But when we talk about remote work and remote teams today, most of us are discussing the movement away from the traditional office. And if that's our frame of reference, then we should probably use 1973 as our official start date. That was the year Jack Nilles published *The Telecommunications-Transportation Tradeoff*. Nilles and his coauthors were convinced that the rising problem of traffic congestion wouldn't be solved by widening highways. Instead, they saw it as a communication problem that technology was rapidly solving. They argued that companies could help ease the traffic problem by shrinking the size of their headquarters and building an array of satellite offices scattered at the edges of their home city — which isn't all that different from remote workers scattered around an array of local coffee shops today. There weren't any personal computers at the time, and the coffee wasn't as good, but Nilles and company believed that mainframe computer technology and existing telephone lines were sufficient to coordinate work remotely. Nilles even coined a term for this: telework.

The advocates for telework only grew stronger as technology advanced and computers shrank in size. In 1989, Charles

Handy argued that personal telephones signaled the beginning of the end for large offices, writing, "Link it to a laptop computer and a portable fax, and a car or a train seat becomes an office." In 1993, fellow management thinker Peter Drucker declared, "Commuting to the office is obsolete." But corporate leaders must not have gotten the fax. And if they did, giving up their corner office wasn't something they wanted to rush into. Instead of an office-less revolution, the percentage of remote workers increased slowly. It grew most quickly among tech firms, perhaps because of their familiarity with the very tools needed to more effectively collaborate from afar.

In the past decade, two big events shaped the debate about remote teams and whether "working from home" was actually just a form of barely working. The first occurred in February 2013, when newly appointed Yahoo! CEO Marissa Mayer sent a companywide memo declaring the end of remote work for the company. "We need to be one Yahoo!" the memo read. "And that starts with physically being together." Many companies followed suit. Hewlett Packard, IBM, and even Best Buy (previously known for its "Results-Only Work Environment") all called their remote teams back from home to the home office. In lieu of working remotely, many of these same tech companies increased their lavish spending on workplace "perks" designed to not so subtly encourage employees to focus more on their work and less on worrying about the outside world.

And so the remote-work revolution's pace slowed to a

crawl. By 2018, only around 3 percent of American employees reported that they worked more than half of their hours remotely. The march toward remote work was still growing, but much more slowly than before.

Then, suddenly, it got an unexpected push. The response to the threat of the COVID-19 pandemic practically brought the world to its knees, but it brought movement toward remote work to an all-out sprint. At the time, moving everyone rapidly to remote teams was reactionary and likely seen as temporary. But having sampled the benefits of remote work, most people don't want to go back to the office any time soon.

A survey conducted by IBM during the height of the COVID-19 pandemic found that more than half of employees want remote work to be their primary method of working, and 75 percent said they'd like the option to continue working remotely at least some of the time. And many companies have responded in kind. Partly out of safety concerns and partly in response to what they discovered during their forced trial of remote work, many companies announced that they would give employees the ability to continue working remotely long after efforts to "flatten the curve" of COVID-19 cases was over. Citigroup, one of the world's largest banks, told its people that most of them would be staying out of the office for nearly a year. Facebook CEO Mark Zuckerberg went even further, announcing that likely half of their 48,000 employees would shift to remote work permanently. (The Facebook announcement is particularly ironic, because during the height of the "office perks" trend, the company spent more than $1 billion and hired renowned architect Frank Gehry to create the largest open office floor plan in the world.) Like Hayden Brown, Shopify CEO Tobi Lütke announced that Canada's most valuable company would become a "digital-by-default" company. They'd keep some of their office space for some operations, but the move to remote was permanent. "Office centricity is over."

The COVID-19 pandemic and response will be remembered for a lot of things, almost all of them tragedies. But it will also be seen as the push needed to get the remote-work movement to critical mass. Now that most managers have seen firsthand the benefits and challenges of remote work, most have recognized that the rewards significantly outweigh the risks — and will only continue to do so as developments in technology decrease those risks.

When you look at the research, remote workers and teams are more productive than office-bound employees and, properly managed, more engaged as well. In 2014, one year after Marissa Mayer's infamous memo, Stanford economist Nicholas Bloom was presented with an intriguing research opportunity that would change a lot of our thinking about remote work. He was approached by graduate student James Liang, who was also a cofounder of the Chinese travel website Ctrip, at the time a sixteen-thousand-person, NASDAQ-listed company. Liang told Bloom that Ctrip was investigating letting call center employees work from home but wanted to make sure they ran the experiment right.

Under Bloom's guidance, Ctrip gave employees in a specific department within the call center the chance to volunteer to work from home for nine months. The company required at least six months' tenure and a dedicated room at home with high-speed internet access: 249 expressed interest and fit the requirements. From there, the volunteers were divided into two groups. Half were asked to stay put in the office as a control group, and the other half were set up with the same technological equipment as the office workers so that they could follow the same workflow processes and be evaluated for their performance on the same metrics. Essentially, the only thing that changed was the location of the work.

So what happened at the end of the nine months? "The results we saw at Ctrip blew me away," recalled Bloom. When they examined the data, Bloom and Liang found that people working from home had completed 13.5 percent more calls than the office staff did, while also taking fewer work breaks and sick days during the nine-month period. "Meaning that Ctrip got almost an extra workday a week out of them," Bloom explained. In addition, employees who worked from home quit at half the rate of employees who commuted to the office each day to work the phones.

In looking for an explanation for the dramatic increase in performance, Bloom and Liang found that it wasn't so much that working from home boosted performance as it was that working from an office *decreased* performance. They estimated that one-third of the productivity increase of the at-home employees was likely the result of a quieter environment having made it easier to process the calls, and the other two-thirds was purely based on putting in more time. Without a commute into an office full of distractions, employees started earlier, took shorter breaks, didn't leave the office to run errands during lunch, and worked until the end of each day. "At home, people don't experience what we call the 'cake in the break room' effect," Bloom said. At least for Ctrip, the office turned out to be a terrible place to get work done.

Research like this proves what you likely suspected already. Ask anyone who works in a company office where they go when they "really" need to get work done and they rarely mention their office — especially if it's one of those open offices where their desk is really just a seat at a long table or a low-walled cubicle and their office door is actually a pair of noise-canceling headphones. Odd, isn't it? We built large and elaborate spaces so that everyone could work together, only to find that, much of the time, everyone being together is just a distraction when trying to get work done.

Besides the freedom to focus and reduced (or nonexistent) commute time, much of that productivity and retention is driven by increases in employee engagement when people shift to remote work. The Gallup organization, one of the global leaders in employee engagement surveys, has been studying engagement in the context of remote work since 2008. In its 2020 State of the American Workplace study, released just before the reality of the COVID-19 pandemic hit American shores, Gallup found that having the option to work remotely significantly increased employees' likelihood of reporting that they were engaged in their work — but only to a point. The optimal engagement boost from working remotely happened when employees spent between 60 and 80 percent of their time off-site — that is, three or four days out of the week.

It's difficult to predict, at the time of this writing, what the post-pandemic future of work looks like in its entirety. But it's not difficult to see that the prevalence of remote work isn't going back to Yahoo!-memo levels any time soon. Instead, most employees whose jobs can allow it will likely become remote employees to some degree — splitting their time between the office, the home, the coffee shop, and wherever else they want. Others may find themselves working for a distributed company — one so remote that there isn't even an office to go to. Taking all of the research on productivity and engagement together, all leaders should be developing a plan to make their work arrangements permanently flexible. Many employees will be permanently working from anywhere; which means you need a plan to lead from anywhere.

This book is that plan. It offers you specific insights, ideas, tools, tactics, and techniques for leading remote teams. In the pages that follow (or the pixels or sound waves — let's be fair to all book formats), we'll cover the full range of what leaders need to know about teamwork in the remote-work era. And we'll do so by examining the complete life cycle of a remote team.

We'll start in chapter 1 with what to do when your team is going remote, whether your team is transitioning to remote work or whether you've newly been appointed the leader of a remote team. And we'll cover how to establish shared expectations about working together as well as build a shared identity around the team.

Chapter 2 challenges a lazy assumption about team culture: that it's largely in-office perks and benefits. Instead, many companies that have been remote from their beginnings have become renowned for their strong and positive company cultures — and we'll explore what they did and how you can do it, too.

Chapter 3 reveals how to properly add new members to your remote team, making sure you hire the right people and that they feel included, even if they haven't met their colleagues on the other end of all those pixels in a video call.

Chapter 4 focuses on making sure your remote teammates, newly hired or not, feel connected to one another and aligned with the team. Remote work can get lonely, but the best remote teams build bonds that are often even stronger than in-person teams.

Chapter 5 is a deep dive into how to communicate with

those teammates. We'll review the different types of communication and examine best practices for each medium — and always with a focus on getting work *done,* not just talking about it.

Chapter 6 goes even deeper into one of the most commonly used methods of team communication: team meetings. We'll cover the opportunities and challenges presented by remote-team meetings and offer a method to ensure that your virtual meetings run better than "real" ones.

Chapter 7 covers problem-solving and creative thinking in remote teams. While we tend to assume that generating ideas is the job of lone, creative individuals, in reality creativity is a team sport. And it's no different for remote teams.

Chapter 8 rethinks performance management — or really just rethinks our lazier management habits. Management in a remote era means abandoning the idea that presence equals productivity. Instead, smart team leaders know how to help their people establish measurements that matter, and that matters even more in remote work.

Chapter 9 examines the other side of staying productive: silencing distractions. The best remote-team leaders help their people establish boundaries between remote work and the rest of their life even when things get blurry. That not only limits distractions but helps prevent burnout as well.

And in chapter 10 we'll consider the most difficult challenge any team (remote or otherwise) faces: saying goodbye. No team lasts forever, and the best team leaders help their people stay connected to their colleagues while also helping them get ready to thrive on their next team.

In case we don't answer all your questions in these ten chapters, we've also included two sections at the end of the book. The first offers a brief rundown of the various technologies you may need to lead your team, and the second serves as a catch-all for any questions you might have that were too big to be ignored but didn't fit into an existing chapter. You're welcome to read this book from chapter 1 to chapter 10 or jump around to different chapters to find the right ideas for the situation you are currently facing.

It all adds up to what you'll need to survive and thrive as the leader of a remote team — which is something all leaders will need to consider themselves from now on.

1

GOING REMOTE

Whether you're leading a new team in a remote company or you're charged with taking your in-person team remote, your team's success or failure depends on a few key elements. Even before you've settled on what software to use, get your team to a place of shared understanding, shared identity, and shared purpose.

THE MINUTE WE shut our door, we stopped producing any revenue."

Curtis Christopherson never planned to lead remote teams or work with clients remotely. But all that changed when the COVID-19 crisis forced his business to shutter. Suddenly Christopherson, the founder and CEO of Innovative Fitness, was watching his in-person training model get thrown out the window. Innovative Fitness was celebrating its twenty-fifth anniversary just as it was making plans to close the doors to every one of its twelve locations. At the start of 2020, the company employed more than 250 personal trainers and support personnel. Each of those trainers worked out of a physical location that had a reputation for drawing in clients. "If you're staying at the Ritz-Carlton in Toronto and want a personal training session, the concierge sends you to us. That's how similar the quality of our customer experience is."

Innovative Fitness's entire revenue depended on in-person interactions in a world where in-person interactions were suddenly scarce. As the novel coronavirus pandemic grew uncontainable, Christopherson knew his company would need to change fast.

When he was informed that a few people and a couple of clients had come back from a trip to Europe and tested positive for the coronavirus, Christopherson didn't hesitate. That very night, Sunday, March 15, he scheduled an all-hands videoconference and told everyone they wouldn't be opening the next day. He didn't know what they would do, but he did know they weren't going to unknowingly contribute to the virus's spread. Christopherson told his employees that they would be paid in full through the end of that week and that the company would have a full plan ready to go by then as well. "We told them, 'We'll figure it out and we'll get back to you by Friday.' And then we put our heads together and tried to find that plan." They looked at best-case scenarios of being closed for a few weeks and worst-case scenarios of being closed for six months. And they looked at pivoting the entire business.

They chose to pivot.

They chose to go remote.

The company was already working with a software provider to develop a proprietary system for appointment scheduling and billing. They reached out and asked a wild question: "Can you add video calling to the platform?" When their provider said yes, they had their plan. They would create — in two weeks — an entire system for their personal trainers to meet virtually with their existing clients and keep the relationships (and revenue) going. They also created a curriculum not only to teach their trainers how to use the software but also to effectively train remote clients — software they were still in the process of building. And they created template workout plans that could be used with no equipment in a variety of home environments.

On that Friday, one week into their two-week transformation, Christopherson again met online with his entire staff. He told them, "We're going to offer the same quality of service and the same training schedule to all of our clients. Nothing is going to change except how we meet to train them." Christopherson also leaned heavily on the company's existing mission and vision and stressed how understanding they were of each employee's situation because of the crisis. But at the end of the meeting he asked a simple question: "Are you in?"

"Out of approximately 225 trainers, 205 said yes right away," Christopherson recalled.

On March 30, Innovative Fitness launched its virtual personal training service with a team of fully trained virtual fitness instructors.

While a majority of their in-person clients have now returned to the studio, the virtual offering is still Innovative Fitness's fastest-growing revenue source — and it's not going away.

Christopherson reflected on how large — and overdue — this shift felt. "What's craziest to me is that we had totally ignored basically all technology. We had a website, but it was barely optimized," he explained. "In the twenty-five years we'd been in existence, we'd never converted a single website visitor to a client without them coming into a location and talking to one of us." Once they launched their virtual offering, they started seeing customers all over the world sign up, with very little interaction needed. Having a remote division of the company has allowed Innovative Fitness to find clients anywhere at any time, but it's also allowed them to hire and retain talent from all over the world. In the past, if a trainer moved outside of their geographic footprint, that was the end of the relationship. Now Innovative Fitness can keep them on as part of the team.

Instead of a brick-and-mortar company with a virtual training offering, Christopherson now considers Innovative Fitness a remote company that happens to own a few gyms. "We're striving to become the Uber of personal training. Anywhere you are in the world, we can connect you with a fitness instructor to guide you through a custom-tailored workout based on your goals, needs, abilities, and equipment."

Christopherson may not have planned on one day leading a remote company. But now he's got no plans to go back.

Many of the challenges Christopherson and Innovative Fitness faced are shared by every leader tasked with managing a remote team. They had to figure out how to train clients in a virtual environment, but, more important, they had to figure out how to train more than two hundred employees to work together and with their clients entirely remotely. That's your primary challenge as a remote leader as well, and one that's critical to the success of a remote business: helping the team learn to work together without face-to-face interaction.

Whether a new crisis has mandated that your team go remote, or you've just become the leader on an already remote team, "going remote" creates a lot of obstacles beyond simple logistics.

How do you make people feel like a team when they're not physically together?

How do you help them collaborate when they can't just walk to each other's cubicles?

How do you keep them aligned and motivated to the task at hand, even when they're working in different time zones or juggling responsibilities at home?

Fortunately, while remote work might be new for a lot of organizations, remote teams have existed in some form for long enough that we can learn an incredible amount from their successes and setbacks. Martine Haas and Mark Mortensen have been studying remote teams for years — including global ones made up of members from a cross section of an organization (a truly "boundaryless" type of team if ever there was one). They have seen how going remote can create a host of challenges and opportunities for teams and their leaders. But two elements in particular stood out as unique challenges that leaders need to address whether their existing team is going remote *or* they're just forming a new team in a remote environment: *shared understanding* of one another's work habits and environment and *shared identity* among the team.

In this chapter we'll look at how to accomplish each in turn and offer a third element that's important and urgent for managers of all types of teams: uniting your team around a shared purpose.

Shared Understanding

In the traditional models of how teams develop, there's a controlled chaos in the early moments of the team's life. One prominent model even calls the first stage after a team forms "storming," because team members are voicing their opinions and feeling one another out, so conflict is a given until the team gradually settles into norms of behavior and everyone learns about the others' working habits. Most of these models were developed for in-person teams, where teams can move through this stage rapidly. In a remote team, it falls to the leader to bring about these norms while minimizing the conflict. That's where shared understanding comes in.

Shared understanding refers to the extent to which members of the team have a commonly held perspective on the team's expertise, assigned tasks, context, and preferences. Different members of the team have different skills, abilities, and knowledge. On a remote team, it's likely that they'll also come from different cultural contexts and different contextual constraints. While this may also be true of in-person teams, the chances of being misunderstood or misinterpreted are higher in a remote team, which lacks the influence of a shared environment. Team members need to know who knows what, who's taking on what responsibility, and also how to approach each person with requests for help — or *offers* of help, for that matter. Providing team members with space to develop this shared understanding is crucial.

One simple way to get started is to build in purposefully unstructured time during team meetings or elsewhere in the week to discuss a wide range of topics. Giving the team space to talk about daily life events, family moments, or even industry news unrelated to the task at hand provides each team member with an opportunity to learn more about the others. Haas and Mortensen even recommend letting team members give "virtual tours" of their workspaces by panning the camera around the room during a video call and showing their remote-team members the environment they work in (including what distractions they are dealing with and how they stay productive).

Another simple approach to shared understanding is coordinating calendars. The location-free nature of teams gives everyone freedom to design a calendar that works for them. But it's best if those calendars have a little bit of overlap in them. Having to work together on projects with a full day's delay can get tiresome. And unless you're a truly global team, it's a burden you don't have to bear. So, while you're setting shared expectations with the team, guide them to a place where everyone's calendar has at least a few hours of overlap to make it possible to jump on a quick call or exchange a few notes throughout the day.

Along with shared understanding comes equal access to infrastructure and developing an understanding of each other's technological capabilities. Remote teams rely on technology, and it's the team leader's role to make sure that team members have equal access to the technologies they'll need to collaborate. Consider how much Innovative Fitness needed to consider on behalf of its employees (and clients) before it could launch its virtual offering and know it would succeed. Likewise, you need to figure out who needs what, and also who needs the training to use those tools. And don't neglect yourself when it comes to that training—it's hard to run an effective virtual meeting when you keep forgetting how to unmute yourself.

This includes not just the technology, but access to information. Make sure your people have access to everything they need. Many companies adopt a "need to know" policy toward information and access to software. With the exception of human resources information, most companies have much less truly sensitive information than they might think. But in an effort to lock down the little bit that is sensitive, companies often unknowingly lock employees out of the information needed to do their job well. In an office environment, this is a mere inconvenience—employees have to track down the person responsible for granting access and wait while they enable it. In a remote environment, it can be downright production-blocking —finding the right person might be easy, but waiting on them to grant access can take days (or longer), because everyone is working asynchronously.

And if you can't default to trusting your employees, then you've got bigger problems to solve than whether or not to give them a username and password.

Developing shared understanding makes coordinating roles easier and collaboration faster. It's a crucial first step in bringing a remote team together or taking an existing team remote. But it's not the only step.

Shared Identity

Developing shared identity is important for any team — but especially for remote ones. Shared identity refers to the extent to which team members feel the same sense of who they are as a designated group. It indicates whether or not individual members truly feel like this is the team they're a part of and most loyal to. Decades of social science research have shown that individuals make sense of their world by applying categories and labels to their environment — including themselves and the people around them. "Team" is one such label, and it carries great importance, because when we identify with a particular group, that group shapes our own identity and behavior.

A strong shared identity in a team reduces conflict, standardizes norms of behavior, increases cohesion and collaboration, and ultimately enhances team performance. But in a remote environment where one or two members of the team are located together and others are scattered, an individual's sense of team can be distorted. Humans have a tendency toward "us versus them" thinking, and the "us" can easily be misinterpreted as in-person team members or even employees in a different function in the organization who happen to work in the same location.

One potent example comes to mind from early in my career, when I worked in sales on a remote "team." The organizational chart defined my team as the nine people who all reported to the same district sales manager. However, the company had two other representatives working in the same territory as me and calling on the same customers (though, thankfully, selling different products). In that blurry context, it was impossible to distinguish which team I was really a part of. Was it the people who all shared the same boss? Or the ones I'd call for help because they lived in the same city, shared the same problem clients, and responded to requests much faster?

I still don't know the answer to that question twenty years later, but I do know who still gets a Christmas card every year — and it's not my old boss.

Deliberately developing shared identity eliminates that confusion. One powerful way to develop not just a team identity but a bond between team members is to point to (and continue pointing to) the team's superordinate goal. Superordinate goals are the objectives that affect everyone in a group (or across groups) and that require participation from everyone affected in order to be achieved. They can be a goal, but they can also be a challenge — a challenge that threatens everyone in the team unless that team comes together to take it on. For Innovative Fitness, that primary goal was just ensuring that the organization would survive, but even now they lean heavily on the company's mission and values of using personalized fitness to help people live their best lives.

Studies of superordinate goals show that when multiple

groups are brought together and tasked with something that requires them to choose between collaboration and failure — they choose collaboration more often. In doing so, they choose to redefine their team not as the original group but as the newly formed team of teams. And that new identity lingers as long as the superordinate goal is out there.

Superordinate goals may be the key to smashing silos and ending turf wars throughout an organization. And for a remote team, superordinate goals are the secret to shared identity. When you're discussing roles and responsibilities, or even just checking progress, make sure you connect individual efforts back to the superordinate goal. Whenever you're talking about individual productivity, take the time to point back to the larger "why?" your team is working for. Remind individuals that their individual efforts are progress toward a larger mission, and be prepared to share stories of how even the smallest wins for your team were milestones toward that mission.

It's tricky to know if your team's performance objectives alone are large enough to become the superordinate goal that creates shared identity. That's why in recent years I've taken an unorthodox approach with the companies and leaders I work with to ensure goals are seen as superordinate. It all has to do with how we talk about the larger purpose.

Shared Purpose

We know that people want a sense of purpose, and they want it for more than just their personal lives. They want it at work as well. But we also have to admit that a lot of organizations stumble in portraying that purpose in a way that helps their people feel *their* job is truly important.

One of the core questions at the heart of Gallup's renowned Q12 employee engagement survey asks employees whether or not the mission or purpose of the company makes their job feel important. And in response to all that talk about mission, organizations large and small have taken the time to craft their "perfect" mission or vision statement. Or both.

And yet in the twenty years since Gallup started administering the survey, the percentage of engaged employees has hovered between the mid-twenties and the low thirties the entire time. To me this suggests that the disconnect lies between the stated mission or purpose of an organization and an individual employee's role in the company. One reason for that disconnect could be that the mission statement sucks — who wants to hear all about "shareholder value" other than shareholders? But it could also be because leaders don't take the time to communicate how individual roles, or even specific teams, help get the mission accomplished. In other words, the company mission doesn't get actively translated into a team's shared mission or shared vision.

As I've worked with more organizations and teams about establishing a shared purpose, I've developed a litmus test of sorts for whether or not the overall mission of the organization has been internalized. I look for a clear and concise answer to this question:

"What are we fighting for?"

Not "*Who* are we fighting?" That's a question about competitors and sets up an us-versus-them competitive mindset that likely won't be useful. "What are we fighting for?" might mean "What is the problem in the world we're trying to solve?" or "What is the injustice in the world we're working to resolve?" or even just "What are we trying to prove?"

Now, before you dismiss the idea as too violent or old-fashioned, let me just say that I get it. Corporations have used battle language for decades, in vain attempts to rally their employees, and found it wanting. But that's largely for the reason we discussed above: they've focused their "fight" rhetoric on competitors, many times the very organizations employees just came from or will work for in a few years' time. And even if not, it's not effective because it's a short-term mentality.

We're talking about longer-term purpose.

And so, when I ask teams "What are we fighting for?" I am checking to see if they've translated the organization's stated purpose in their minds to something larger — something that would even be seen as the superordinate goal discussed previously. It defines, in short, precise language, why the organization exists. And it gives the people inside the organization something most of us deeply want from our work. One of Innovative Fitness's core values is "We find a way. No excuses." When the COVID-19 crisis started, that little line turned into a companywide fight.

Inside the question of "What are we fighting for?" there are three templates or types of "fights" that research suggests are most inspiring to individuals and create a shared purpose in teams:

- The revolutionary fight
- The underdog fight
- The ally fight

The revolutionary fight is about changing the status quo. It's about pointing to something in the industry or in society that your organization and team are working to change. The underdog fight is about taking on the established players in an industry and winning through a better way of operating. And the ally fight isn't actually about a company's fight at all; it's about the customers' or stakeholders' fight and how your work helps them win their battle.

People don't want to join a company; they want to join a crusade.

And as a leader, the best way to build the shared purpose that creates a shared identity and even leads to developing a shared understanding is to point to that crusade early and often and continuously remind people how the work they're doing is advancing the cause.

Establishing these key mindsets early on will set your team up for success. Help your teammates develop a shared understanding of one another's knowledge, skills, strengths, and situations. Likewise, lead them to a shared understanding of the expectations they have for each other. And create a shared identity by appealing to the superordinate goals your team is pursuing and the cause they are fighting for. You won't just make your remote team more productive — you'll make them feel closer to one another, no matter how far away they are.

RULES FOR REMOTE LEADERS

When an existing team goes remote or a new remote team comes into existence, it will face a lot of challenges and opportunities. But leaders' actions when going remote can set that team up for success by responding to those challenges and leveraging those opportunities. Here's a quick review of our rules for remote-team leaders:

- Foster shared understanding by making space for self-disclosure.
- Create shared identity by appealing to superordinate goals.
- Develop shared purpose by answering the question "What are we fighting for?"

And if you're looking for tools to help implement these rules with your team, you can get several resources, like templates, worksheets, videos, and more, at davidburkus.com/resources.

2

BUILDING CULTURE REMOTELY

Culture refers to the unspoken beliefs, values, behaviors, and norms inside an organization. A team's culture will have a dramatic effect on its success or failure, and an even more profound effect on your sanity as team leader. Fortunately, there is considerable research we can use as a blueprint for building team culture.

WHEN FRANK VAN MASSENHOVE was interviewing to become the head of the Belgian Ministry of Social Security, he said what he thought he needed to say to land the job. He said that he would maintain the status quo. He said he wouldn't disrupt much. And it worked. He took the job as head of the organization in 2002, and immediately the reality of what he was taking on struck him. He found a neglected organization spread out over four federal buildings in Brussels.

In one of those buildings, the office space his people occupied had been converted from an old garage, with just minimal up-dates to the building. You could have driven cars through the hallways, because that's what used to happen before desks were put in them. It was a dead-end department for underperform-ing civil servants and citizens who couldn't get a job anywhere else. But the dismay that Van Massenhove inherited was also a tremendous opportunity — and he recognized this right from the start.

"I lied during my interviews," Van Massenhove recalled. "If I was completely honest about my plan not to take all the de-cisions myself and give employees the power, I wouldn't have been appointed." Because the ministry's reputation for poor performance was so bad, no one had any real expectations. In fact, no one was really even watching them. "We kept the door shut for a while, turned it all inside out, and then reopened," he explained.

What did turning it all inside out look like?

The first steps involved giving people autonomy. In the past, the ministry had been run like a lot of people would imagine a government bureaucracy is run. Command-and-control lead-ership style. Very specific prescriptions on when you had to work and how you had to work. But Van Massenhove felt his people didn't need any of that. They may have needed to be told what to do, but they didn't need to be told how to do it. Or even when to do it. "We don't believe in the time clock," he once boasted. "The time clock means that there is a serious possibility that you are in the building." And in Van Massenhove's view, that's all it meant. It didn't mean you were necessarily working.

Giving his people autonomy very quickly came to mean trusting them to work wherever they wanted as well. Once people could extend their work into typical off-hours, and vice versa, the desire naturally followed to be able to get in a few hours of work after putting the kids to bed or when waiting at the dentist's office, and the desire grew from there. In a few years' time, Van Massenhove had transformed a stuffy government bureaucracy with crowded desks in a dank office space into an almost entirely remote organization. Of the 1,200 people employed by the ministry, more than a thousand of them worked mostly remotely during Van Massenhove's tenure. All employees were encouraged to come into the office for a short time every few weeks to check in with each other. But otherwise they were trusted to manage their own schedule and work whatever day, time, and place they wanted.

What was the effect of all that trust?

In the first three years of his tenure, productivity rose 18 percent. After that, it kept rising by an average of around 10 percent per year. The ministry had the lowest number of sick days of any of the Belgian ministries and virtually no burnout. It also won the Gender Balanced Leadership Award for having more balanced representation at all levels of the organization, without having put in place any formal gender policy. More important, the organization transformed in the mind of most civil servants from dead end to most desired place to work. Before Van Massenhove took over, the ministry received only three applications for the average open position. By the end of his tenure, there were close to sixty applicants vying for the same vacancy.

It's not the remote-work element that's attracting all that fresh talent and motivating them to be productive. Of course, that helps, but, more important, it's the culture that Van Massenhove built inside the ministry — or, more accurately, rebuilt. "We provide evidence that a culture based on freedom and trust really does work," Van Massenhove argued. "We do the same work, but the way we do it is different."

Van Massenhove sought to build a thriving organizational culture inside the ministry, and the result was that the ministry transformed into a remote organization. But even if your team is already remote (even if it has been for some time), that foundational step of building (or rebuilding, as the case may be) the right culture can be the difference between your team thriving and not thriving. So in this chapter, we'll cover what makes for a thriving team culture and offer several tactics you can use to build (or rebuild) that culture on your remote team.

What We Talk About When We Talk About Culture

A company's culture might seem tough to pinpoint, but we experience it every day, and it heavily influences how we feel about the work we're doing and our role in the organization. A company's culture reflects the predominant way its people think and act. But it's also about how a company's people treat one another every day. As the migration from in-person teams to remote teams increases, company culture as an overarching influence (from the top down) becomes less relevant, and the relevance of individual team culture increases. That means that, as a remote leader, the burden of building culture falls on you.

Fortunately, we now have solid research on the key elements needed to create the best team culture.

In 2015, Google's People Analytics team asked an ambitious question: "Why do some teams perform better than others?" The Googlers (as they're called) partnered with some of the best organizational psychologists and statisticians in the world to perform one of the largest studies of teams ever conducted. At first, they thought it came down to who was on the team and that getting the right people in the right seats was all it took. But the data didn't produce any discernible patterns when it came to people. It wasn't about how talented individual members were or whether the right mix of skills, abilities, and knowledge existed. "We looked at 180 teams from all over the company," explained Abeer Dubey, who helped lead the project for Google. "We had lots of data, but there was nothing showing that a mix of specific personality types or skills or backgrounds made any difference. The 'who' part of the equation didn't seem to matter."

But when the researchers turned their attention from the attributes of the team toward its regular behaviors, traditions, and norms (in other words, its culture), they started to find patterns that really did explain the difference between the highest-performing teams and everyone else. In total, they found five elements of a team's culture that seemed to explain how the best teams became the best teams:

- Dependability: The extent to which team members were accountable to shared expectations.
- Structure and clarity: Whether the team had established roles and rules of engagement.
- Meaning: How much the team felt their work had significance.
- Impact: How much the team felt their work made a difference.
- Psychological safety: How much the team felt they could be vulnerable and authentic with one another.

Some of this we've already covered. As you'll recall from the last chapter, Martine Haas and Mark Mortensen found that virtual teams struggled to be effective when they failed to develop shared understanding and shared expectations. (In other words, they lacked dependability, structure, and clarity.) And my own research suggests that teams bond most effectively when they can answer the question "What are we fighting for?" (when they develop a shared meaning and sense of impact around the work they are doing). But we haven't yet explored that fifth element that vitally contributes to a thriving team culture: psychological safety.

So what are we talking about when we talk about psychological safety? Amy Edmondson, the foremost researcher on the topic, described it as "a team climate characterized by interpersonal trust and mutual respect in which people are comfortable being themselves."

In one experiment, Edmondson examined the leadership of charge nurses on different floors of a hospital and noticed that nurses who were judged by their teams as being better leaders often had higher rates of documented errors than those who were judged to be worse leaders. But as she began investigating further, she quickly discovered an explanation. It wasn't about the mistakes; it was about the documentation. The better leaders created psychological safety, so that the nurses on that ward felt free to admit to their mistakes and receive correction, and then everybody could benefit from the learning that happened after the mistake. When poor leaders didn't create enough psychological safety, the individual nurses felt like they had to hide their mistakes. Beyond the ethical issues, hiding mistakes also meant that those teams were deprived of that learning.

Psychological safety is the measure of how free people on the team are to share their ideas, their experiences, and their whole selves with their team. Psychological safety helps team members be more willing to submit crazy ideas that might lead the team in a different direction, but a direction that ultimately leads to genius.

So how do we build psychological safety into the culture of our team? If we look back at Edmondson's definition, it seems to depend on two key elements:

Interpersonal trust and mutual respect.

If you want to build a culture of psychological safety on your team (and why wouldn't you, given that we just identified it as the last element of a thriving team culture?), then you've got to focus on developing a climate of trust and respect. Let's look at each concept in turn.

Trust

The first building block of psychological safety is trust. I know it may sound cliché at this point, because you've heard it so often, but in a way, that underscores just how true it is that the core element of healthy, productive cultures for both companies and teams is trust. If members of the team trust one another and trust their leader, almost everything runs more smoothly. Research on high-trust organizations shows that they report 74 percent less stress and 106 percent more energy at work than low-trust organizations. They have 76 percent more engagement, are 50 percent more productive, and take 13 percent fewer sick days. And individuals who work for high-trust organizations experience 26 percent more satisfaction with their lives and 40 percent less burnout.

We've all heard about the importance of trust, but the difficulty comes in actually building trust on your team. Remote or not, trust often feels frustratingly intangible. How do you measure this quality in your team? How do you know you have it yourself? It turns out that much of our difficulty understanding trust might stem from thinking it's a feeling or an emotion.

But trust is a chemical.

Specifically, trust is felt by humans when the chemical oxytocin is more present in the brain and the bloodstream. Oxytocin is produced by your body naturally; it's a peptide, a chain of amino acids, if you want to get nerdy. In fact, it's often called the "bonding hormone," since it's released when you're engaged in strong bonding activities. When mothers give birth or nurse their babies, oxytocin increases. When we hug, touch, or even enjoy meals with others, oxytocin increases. When oxytocin is present, our heart rate reduces, respiration lowers, and stress hormones decrease. Interestingly, our brain's attention, memory, and error recognition increase. For all these reasons (and a few more), scientists who study oxytocin believe it not only reduces fear but increases trust between individuals.

In one study, researcher Paul Zak wanted to examine whether increasing participants' oxytocin would increase their perception of trust and whether or not they would act in a trustworthy manner when engaging with others. To do this, Zak and his team modified a commonly used laboratory experiment run by economists: the investment game. In the standard version, participants are paired up randomly with an anonymous partner. Player one in the game is given $10 and told that he can give any amount to player two, including $0. Both players are told that any amount transferred will be tripled. So if player one sends $5 to player two, player two will actually receive $15. And in the last step, player two is told that she can give any amount back to player one, including $0. (This is where the "investment" part of the name comes from. Player one is "investing" in player two and trusting her to give a positive return.)

Logically, this game should produce zero investment. Player one is asked to trust that player two, whom he's never met, will send back some portion of the newly tripled amount. But player two could just as easily take the money and run. Player one should anticipate this, take the money, and run first.

But that's rarely what happens, because humans are a trusting species. And that's what Zak and his team found. When participants had completed the game, with varying degrees of investment, they were escorted to a room to have their blood drawn and tested for oxytocin. Astonishingly, Zak found that the investment choices players made correlated to the level of oxytocin in their blood. The more oxytocin, the more they trusted their partner in the game. And the more player one trusted player two, the more player two felt trusted and responded in kind. "Oxytocin rises when someone trusts you," Zak explained, "and facilitates trustworthiness."

So trust isn't necessarily given, and it's not earned. It's both. **Trust is reciprocated.**

And in the context of leading a remote team — or any team — building trust means creating opportunities for individuals to feel trusted and act in trusting ways. Leaders should seek to create these opportunities on a small scale first, knowing that they will increase over time into a larger sense of trust as the team continues to work together. Start small. And go first. Demonstrate that you trust your team to get their work done without being constantly monitored (we'll cover that in greater depth later) and they'll feel trusted and respond in kind. Share your thoughts and concerns openly and your team will feel trusted with your vulnerability and will respond in kind. Admit mistakes and your team will feel like they can trust you and admit their mistakes to you. Take responsibility for performance concerns and your team will feel like they can do the same, instead of shifting blame somewhere else.

Trust is a huge component of fostering psychological safety. But the other, equally important factor is making sure your team demonstrates respect in every interaction.

Respect

While trust refers to the degree to which I can share my authentic self with you, respect refers to the level I feel that you accept that self. If I trust you, it means that I will be open with you when I share. If you respect me, it means you value what I share.

Unfortunately, respect in the workplace — or at least *feeling* respected in the workplace — is shockingly low, despite the enormous impact it has on organizations. In a 2013 survey of more than twenty thousand workers, Georgetown University professor Christine Porath and researcher Tony Schwartz found that 54 percent of respondents claimed they don't regularly get respect from their leaders. That lack of respect translated into less engagement, more turnover, less focus and productivity, fewer feelings of meaning and significance, and even greater healthcare costs for the organization. In fact, no other variable had a bigger effect on employee outcomes than leaders' demonstration of respect toward their people. Part of the reason that leaders' respect toward employees is so important is that it's contagious.

Respect is a learned behavior.

Porath's research has found that incivility and rude behavior have a contagion effect on all of us. Observing a disrespectful behavior in the morning dampens our mood momentarily, but it can also lower our performance throughout the day and make it much more likely that we — intentionally or not — exhibit a rude behavior toward someone else. Negative emotions ripple out from negative actions and spread through an entire community — or, in our case, team. The good news is that positive emotions and positive actions seem to have the same contagiousness. Which means the best way to build a culture of respect is to model that respect to each member of your team — especially when team members are watching you interact with others.

In fact, a significant portion of the workers Porath has surveyed reported that the reason for their own disrespectful behavior was that they didn't have a role model in the organization to set the standard for how to behave — they were just copying their disrespectful leaders. But the most common reason cited for disrespectful behavior in the workplace is even more shocking and, ultimately, counterproductive. More than 60 percent of workers surveyed in one study Porath conducted cited "lack of time" as their primary reason to ignore civility and act in a disrespectful way. They were just too overloaded and "didn't have time to be nice."

Porath herself is quick to point out that this is a hollow excuse. Respect is about how you conduct yourself during interactions you're going to have anyway. Acting respectfully toward others doesn't require any extra time — just a little bit more conscious attention to your interactions, which will save you lots of headaches down the line. If you think about the last few interactions you had that involved new ideas, opinions, and feedback, was your immediate reaction to push back or challenge when someone's opinion differs from yours? It's perfectly acceptable to disagree, but make sure you demonstrate that you've actually listened and understand their point of view. If you want to change their mind, offer them more information on the concept being discussed rather than challenging the validity of their information. Doing the latter not only will make them feel disrespected, but likely won't change their mind, and they'll retreat further into their camp. If they still disagree with you even after receiving new information, choose curiosity over conflict. Instead of rebuttals, offer questions that help you better understand and reflect on their opinion. These simple swaps keep the lines of communication open, saving you from bigger disagreements down the road.

Be present and attentive when in real-time conversations.

On a video chat, that means making sure to keep the screen your top window, engaging with others, and making eye contact as much as possible. (We'll say more on communicating remotely in a few chapters.) On a phone call, it means taking extra care not to talk over or interrupt others. Without visible cues, it can be difficult to know when someone is truly finished expressing their thought and when they're just taking a breath. So look for that extended pause or, even better, wait for them to ask you what you think of what they just said. And when you do talk, make sure you incorporate everything from the previous paragraph. These little actions have huge positive consequences. When people feel heard and understood, when they feel respected, they're more likely to share new ideas with the whole team, be receptive to feedback on their performance, and exhibit respectful behavior toward the rest of the team. And on a remote team, where real-time conversations are much less frequent, these little actions become a big deal.

Lastly, and perhaps most important, ask for feedback from trusted colleagues. It's a quirk of human nature that many of us are blind to our most offensive slights. So before heading into a meeting that might get heated, ask a teammate you trust to observe and report back anything that might have been misinterpreted as disrespect. Even better, ask that person to keep track of times you were on your best behavior as well, like when you caught yourself before interrupting or how you looked them in the eye when listening to them. You'll likely have quicker wins if you double down on the things you do well than if you try to correct all your blind-spot bad behaviors anyway.

Over time, your emphasis on respectful behavior will be mirrored by everyone on your team. And if not, then you've got a good reason to respectfully invite that problem person to be disrespectful on a new team.

A respectful environment combined with a sense of trust between team members is a solid foundation for building psychological safety. And psychological safety is the cornerstone of a positive culture. If you combine that with a shared understanding, shared expectations, and a firm answer to the question "What are we fighting for?" then you'll be well on your way to creating a thriving team culture that keeps your team productive, engaged, and — let's be honest — just plain fun to lead.

RULES FOR REMOTE LEADERS

Your team's culture will have a dramatic effect on their overall collaboration and performance. Here's a quick review of our rules for remote-team leaders when it comes to building a thriving culture:

- Psychological safety is the core element of thriving team cultures.
- Psychological safety is built on trust and respect.
- Trust is reciprocated.
- Respect is a learned behavior.

And if you're looking for tools to help implement these rules for building positive culture on your team, you can get several resources, like templates, worksheets, videos, and more, at davidburkus.com/resources.

3

HIRING REMOTE TEAMMATES

You've taken your team remote and built a culture around psycho-logical safety, but who you hire next time there's an opening will affect whether your culture stays that way or not — and will have an equally large effect on team performance. Make sure you're choos-ing candidates who not only have the skills for the job but have the right collaboration, communication, and motivation habits to fit the team.

YOU MIGHT HAVE never heard of the software company Automattic. But chances are you've used their product at some point today. (Unless, of course, you're reading this first thing in the morning, in which case: Good morning. Thanks for making me part of your wake-up routine!) The company's main product is a blogging platform called WordPress, which powers more than one-third of all websites on the internet, everything from small personal blogs to major publications like *TechCrunch, People,* and *Vogue.* But Automattic isn't just known for WordPress. It's also known for its unique approach to hiring.

Founded in 2005 by Matt Mullenweg and Mike Little, Automattic now employs more than 1,200 people in seventy-seven countries, speaking ninety-three languages. The vast majority of those employees work remotely, and all of them were put through a hiring process that's brought CEO Mullenweg a lot of attention.

Automattic employees audition for their role.

When he was first building the company, Mullenweg hired in the traditional way. He'd interview the candidates and place them on a team, or sometimes have potential new hires meet with a panel of current employees. But Mullenweg grew increasingly disappointed with that process every time an employee turned out to be a poor fit. "When we hire someone at Automattic," Mullenweg said in an interview with the *Harvard Business Review,* "we want the relationship to last for decades." But at one point, up to one-third of new hires weren't working out and were leaving the company soon after being hired. Obviously, the traditional interview process wasn't leading to relationships that lasted.

So Mullenweg looked to his current employees and took the time to experiment with different ways of sorting the ones who fit the best and lasted the longest. In the end, strong communication skills seemed to be the winning trait. It's a misconception that a mostly remote company means most employees working away in silence and communicating only when necessary. Communication and collaboration become even *more* important in a distributed team. And not just communicating status updates or making comments on a shared document. Receiving and responding to feedback on their own work was a top-tier skill needed by everyone in the company.

Over time, Mullenweg found that the best way to find out who communicated well and who was open to feedback was to let them work alongside their future colleagues — to give them a trial. So, while Automattic's hiring process starts out looking normal, it quickly transforms into something completely unconventional. Candidates have their résumé reviewed, and those who appear qualified undergo a first-round interview. But then, if they seem like a good match, they're placed on a project team and set to work.

They're placed on real teams and work on real projects. They're given the permissions, logins, and security clearances they need to do real work. Engineering candidates start writing real code that might end up in the final product. Design candidates work on real designs for the company's numerous products. Customer service candidates field real requests from puzzled customers.

Because it's a remote company, these candidates work remotely during all hours of the day — which is a huge positive, because many of them do their trial hours before or after their current job that they're hoping to quit soon. All candidates are paid a standard, hourly, fair-market wage. This isn't about getting free work; it's about assessing the person working.

The length of the trial can vary depending on the candidate, the project, and the team. It's not intended to judge the quality of the finished product; it would be unfair to hold non-employees to the performance standard of current employees. Instead, the trial runs for as long as is needed to give the candidate an accurate feel for the company and the company an accurate picture of what it's like to work with the candidate. "Tryouts may not be exactly what the person will be working on once they're hired, but we're looking at a lot of things besides just their work," Mullenweg explained.

At the end of the trial, feedback is gathered from those who worked with the candidate. If that feedback is positive, and the person seems like a fit, an offer is made. For a long time, Mullenweg took the time to interview every single candidate who passed the trial, though he recognized that how well that person worked with the team was most important. He did still want to meet the candidate and be sure that they'd be able to communicate well with *him*, though — so he conducted the final interview in an online chat room, since much of their communication once they become an Automattician would be via text.

At first glance, hiring by trial may seem novel and unusual. But trials have been around in some form or another for a long time. What is an internship if not a chance to give future job candidates a trial with the company and see if they're a fit? Trials are an investment — it's much easier to hold a few video interviews and email an offer letter — but the return on investment is worthwhile. Shortly after moving to trials, the percentage of people who didn't end up working out dropped to just 2 percent. At Automattic, "it's considered an honor to be put on the hiring group," Mullenweg said. "Everyone in the company recognizes that one of the most important decisions you can make is who to bring on the team."

At their core, trials give teams a chance to find answers to the three questions you need to know about potential remote teammates:

- Are they collaborators?
- Are they communicators?
- Are they self-motivated?

Whether your hiring process involves trials or looks radically different, these three questions should be at the forefront of your mind each time you're considering adding someone new to the team.

Are They Collaborators?

Over the past hundred years, as we shifted from industrial work to knowledge work, many people assumed that collaboration would be less important. After all, in a factory, workers use the means of production together. In an office or a remote team, the means of production is between the ears of each and every employee, so it may be tempting to assume that this kind of work lends itself to working in isolation. But when it comes to remote work, the reality is that collaboration becomes even more vital to the success of the individual and the organization.

We've assumed for a long time that individual performance is the result of an individual's knowledge, skills, and abilities. But the more we research, the more we learn that it's not quite that simple. Collaboration and team dynamics have a significant impact on individual performance. The most notable evidence for this is a study of investment analysts led by Harvard Business School professor Boris Groysberg. Investment analysts study an industry, or sometimes even just a group of companies, to generate reports for institutional investors to use when deciding what decisions to make in their portfolios.

Groysberg had seen how fiercely investment banks will compete for top analyst talent — in some cases offering seven-figure salaries and six-figure signing bonuses to those analysts rated as most talented by the very investors who rely on their reporting. Logically, analyzing data and creating these reports should be a fairly solitary task. It requires your past knowledge and your ability to spot trends and shouldn't require much else. So Groysberg and his team started tracking what happened when star analysts took those lucrative job offers and switched from one firm to another. Altogether, the researchers collected nine years of data on more than a thousand analysts who were recognized in the industry's top trade publication, *Institutional Investor*. They especially focused on those analysts who'd changed jobs after being honored.

What they found was surprising. When analysts were recognized as the most talented among their peers, and the recognition led to a job offer and a change of firms, their talent didn't seem to migrate with them. Instead, their performance declined. On average, those who changed jobs saw their performance decline 20 percent — and in most cases it stayed at that lower level even after a period of five years working for the new company. Moreover, when those analysts switched teams, they seemed to drag the performance of their *new* team down as well.

But Groysberg and his researchers found one type of job change that didn't yield such negative effects on performance, and it's the key to understanding why team fit and collaboration are so important: lift-outs. "Lift-out" is an industry term for when a firm doesn't just hire one analyst, but rather the whole team. When whole teams moved firms, they didn't suffer any of the declines in performance seen by solo switchers. Looking at the movement of members on the teams he studied, Groysberg estimated that up to 60 percent of individual performance was actually a result of the resources a company can provide and the team a person can be placed on.

Talent flows from teams.

If you want to get the best out of individuals, you need to make sure they work best with the team they will be joining. That is why Mullenweg and Automattic went to trials, and why you need to build in a system for testing collaboration with job candidates. If you can't run a tryout, at least try to bring as many current team members into the interview process as possible. Especially in a remote team, this new hire won't be working *for* you as an employee who takes direct orders so much as working *with* you as a teammate who works independently toward mutually beneficial objectives. So it just makes sense to let the people who work with new hires be the ones deciding who gets hired.

Here's a few questions you can add to your interviews to get a feel for what candidates would be like on a team:

- What does your ideal team look like? How often do they interact, and how do they treat each other?
- In what type of culture do you feel you do your best work?
- What was it like working on your last team?

- Have you ever been on a team that just didn't work well? What was it like?

Compare the answers to these questions across *all* job candidates, and also compare them with how your current team would answer. Doing so will give you at least a little information to envision how each candidate would work on the team.

Are They Communicators?

Next to collaboration, communication is likely the most influential factor in the success or failure of your team and your new hire. That was true for the world of in-person work, but it's even more true now in a remote-work world. In 2017, Christoph Riedl and Anita Williams Woolley examined the factors that explained the success or failure of teams working remotely. In a controlled study, they recruited 260 software workers from fifty countries and randomized them into fifty-two teams of five. They gave each team the exact same task: to develop a learning algorithm that could recommend the ideal contents of a medical kit for a space flight.

To inspire greater performance on the teams, they offered half the teams cash prizes for doing the best-quality work. And while the money motivated many teams to work harder, it didn't have an effect on the overall quality of their final product. Instead, it came down to only one factor. You guessed it: communication.

Whether or not the teams developed a rhythm of communication that allowed for maximized collaboration and maximized solo focused time was the key factor that affected the team's likelihood of producing the best-quality work. Specifically, teams that developed what Riedl and Woolley called "bursty" communication performed best. They defined bursty communication as bursts of live, synchronous conversation when it mattered, and asynchronous communication that allowed for focused time afterwards. Knowing when to use which seemed to be crucial to great performance.

We'll cover more evidence and best practices for communication in a few chapters. For now, we need to know how capable candidates are of sustaining long-distance communication and how well their communication preferences match our team's existing methods. That makes video interviews preferable to in-person interviews and makes Mullenweg's case for chat-room-based interviews even stronger. If 90 percent of their communication will be in text chats, then that's a more relevant environment than a video interview. If you are doing video interviews, you might consider breaking out a few questions and asking them to pre-record answers in short videos. That not only makes it easier to assess among candidates, but it showcases how well they communicate ideas briefly (and how well they follow instructions if they can't).

In many cases, that also means that one of the old-school holdovers of pre-technology corporate life has new relevance for remote work.

Yep, we're bringing back the cover letter.

Cover letters used to be a vital element of the job application. When sending a résumé based on a vague job description found in the newspaper, it was your one chance to let the mailroom clerk know how to file it and the hiring manager know why they should slow down when reading it. But in an age of online applications with uploaded (and hence permanently sorted and stored) résumés, the cover letter fell out of use in many organizations (and held on in many slower-moving ones). But now the cover letter offers one of the best glimpses into the communication ability of candidates for remote teams.

Looking deeply at the cover letter helps you decide if candidates are strong writers and if they can formulate an argument — the argument for why they're the right candidate. It's about how well they make the case for the job and how easy it is to understand their train of thought. And the cover letter is the first time they've been asked to do both for you and your team.

It's not so much about their command of the English language, or even their ability to consult a thesaurus. What matters isn't how grammatically correct their language is. What matters is how well it fits into your existing team. If your team uses more emojis than adverbs, then your ideal candidate probably isn't the one with an MFA in English literature (unless, of course, her thesis was on emojis in everyday usage). Toward that end, here are a few questions you can ask in your interview (video or text) to gauge how well a candidate's communication preference fits your team's existing style:

- How do you like to keep in touch with team members?
- What type of communication do you prefer?
- Tell me about a time when a colleague completely misunderstood you. How did you resolve it?
- How often did you proactively reach out to team members or your manager at your last job?

Remember that the goal isn't to find the candidate with the best answers. The goal is to find the candidate whose existing communication preferences match those of your team. (Unless, of course, how your team communicates remotely is broken. In which case, we'll fix that in chapter 5.)

Are They Self-Motivated?

The first two factors to consider in a remote candidate have to do with how well they work with their potential new team. But much of remote work is working alone, so the ability to be self-motivated still matters a lot. Remember the Nicholas Bloom and Ctrip study we examined in the introduction? There is one part of the study we haven't covered yet.

After the nine-month work-from-home trial period, which found that remote workers outperformed their in-person counterparts, Ctrip decided to implement a remote-work policy. Except that, instead of randomly assigning those who'd opted into the study to either an in-person or remote group, they gave remote employees the option of coming back to the office or staying at home; they also gave in-person employees the option of working from home. Many of the remote workers chose to come back to the environment of the office. And many of the in-person workers opted to work remotely.

And productivity increased even more.

It turned out the remote working made employees more productive only if they really *wanted* to work from home. If they tried the remote-working lifestyle and found it too difficult to self-motivate, they moved back to the office and were more productive. And likewise, if they dreaded working at the office and felt they were self-motivated enough to work remotely, making the move to home made them more productive as well. The study's results seem fairly basic, but they underscore an overlooked point about hiring for any type of remote work:

How well people can work without being watched has a massive effect on how well they'll work without being watched.

I know. That sounds like the least astounding sentence you've ever read. But unfortunately, many of the hiring processes for in-person teams doesn't really examine self-motivation — and so they will work even worse for remote teams. Often when the topic of motivation comes up, it's a generic "How are you motivated?" question designed to figure out if the company's existing bonus structure is a fit with this new candidate. (And rarely, if ever, do we reexamine whether that bonus structure is a fit for our existing employees — but that rant could be its own book.) Instead we need to examine if candidates have experience putting in a strong effort without any outside influence.

One great way to know if a candidate is self-motivated enough to work remotely is to examine how much they have done it in the past. If they've previously been on, and thrived on, remote teams, that's a strong indication that they're able to motivate themselves to get to work. But if they haven't, there are still other clues. Have they ever worked as a freelancer or contract employee, or owned their own business? Even if they weren't ultimately successful in those endeavors (which is safe to assume, since they're looking for a new job), the reasons are highly variable and may have nothing to do with work ethic. But the experience of doing that type of work likely taught them how to get to work when no one was watching.

If they've never worked remotely or independently, then it's worth examining other aspects of their life where they have to draw from self-motivation. What hobbies do they have? Are those done more often in groups or alone? What new skills have they been working to develop? And how long have they stuck with the difficult work of developing them? You're not looking for one-word answers. Instead you're looking for stories about their past experiences and clues to how they get themselves up and working when no one is there to do it for them.

Toward that end, here are a few questions you can add to your interview to examine how strong their self-motivation truly is, and whether or not it will be enough to thrive on a remote team:

- How do you organize your day-to-day tasks?
- How do you stay motivated when working alone?
- Tell me about a project you took on all by yourself. How did it go?
- How do you limit distractions around you when working?

It's not enough to know that they want to work on a remote team. A lot of people who think the lifestyle of remote work is appealing focus too much on the word "remote" and not enough on the word "work." The goal with these questions is to assess how well they'll work when they're not in regular contact with the team. We're looking to find out how well they can

motivate themselves to get to work without a manager looking over their shoulder. (And, no, you absolutely should not be
planning on remotely looking over their shoulder.)

Skip the Brainteasers

One more thing when it comes to hiring. You might have noticed what's *not* on the list of questions to ask: brainteasers.
Somewhere around the mid-1990s, this odd trend of asking
riddles or puzzles during job interviews developed. Candidates
would be asked questions like:

- Why are manhole covers round? (So they don't fall into
  the manhole.)
- How many piano tuners are there in Chicago? (Eighty-
  three, according to the Yellow Pages, but you're not
  supposed to look it up. Just guess.)

These imaginary puzzles were even compiled into a book
in the early 2000s, titled *How Would You Move Mount Fuji?* It
was meant to teach hiring managers how to incorporate these
riddles — but mostly it just gave job candidates the answers.

The initial intent behind these types of questions might
have been noble, the idea being that you got to peek inside the
thinking process of a prospective candidate — or at least know

that they had a thinking process. But recent research suggests it's basically useless for distinguishing between candidates. In fact, a 2008 study of more than seven hundred participants showed that the only thing these brainteasers may reveal is the level of narcissism and sadism in the hiring manager asking the questions.

So, once and for all, cut out the brainteasers. And if you still have an itch to do them, let someone else do the hiring.

Onboarding Your New Hire

Before we close out this chapter, we should take a quick look at onboarding. Once you've made your decision, how do you bring the new member of the team on board when you don't have the benefit of welcoming them physically? While onboarding tends to be a process driven by human resources and legal, a lot of recent research suggests that these elements are actually the least important part of a new team member's success.

In a study of new hires led by Keith Rollag of Babson College, the information-heavy approach used by most companies to onboard their employees was found to be far less predictive of a new hire's success than how well that person built connections quickly with a wide array of colleagues from various departments. That's not to say these things aren't important. In most cases they're required. But, as Rollag and his colleagues explained, "Our study found that documentation and training were never the differentiating factors" in an employee's success.

So **prioritize connection over documentation.** You've got to get the paperwork done. But it doesn't need to be done at the cost of building a connection between yourself and your new team member, or between the new hire and the rest of the team. You could schedule a welcome video chat for the whole team to meet and greet their new colleague. If synchronous communication isn't an option, have each existing team member write and send a short welcome note and a reason why they're excited to see your new hire join the team. This could be an email, but a series of videos would be even better. If you followed the process above, many of the existing team already met the newbie during the interview process. So ask the team to share what stood out to them. You could even assign new team members a short task that requires them to meet each of their teammates over the course of the day.

Putting connection over documentation also means making sure your new hire gets the resources and technology needed for a fast start. That means making sure any equipment is sent ahead of time and usernames and passwords are generated before the official start date. If your company's policies require that to happen after the start date, you could still prepare a checklist of steps to get them set up properly. Better still, assign another recently hired team member to walk them through the process. Newbies helping newbies is often the best strategy here, since they not only are most familiar with the setup process, but they also remember what it felt like to be new.

And, if you can, adding an in-person component to the onboarding process is a great touch for a new addition to a remote team. Make a plan to be there to welcome and work alongside your new hire in person. Or align their start date with an in-person all-hands meeting. Both can be remarkable ways to join the team. But if you can't make that work, consider sending a care package. It could be full of company swag or, even better, meaningful items selected by each team member.

Lastly, make sure the day begins and ends with a one-on-one with you. Rather than make their concerns known, most new hires actually self-censor their questions in the first few weeks, to avoid looking like that clueless noob to their new team. As the team leader, the burden falls on you to make sure their concerns are addressed and, more important, that they know they can voice any new concerns freely. Call your new hire at the end of their first day and ask them how it went and how they plan to celebrate a job well done. In that same vein, make a plan to meet with new hires at the end of the first month and first quarter to check in and see how positive or negative their onboarding experience has been. Their feedback will be vital to improving the process for future new hires.

Fred Steckler, chief administrative officer of the US Patent and Trademark Office (which manages a surprising number of remote employees) said it best: "On the first day of work every-one is engaged; the job of the manager is to not mess that up."

One of the most pivotal aspects of running a thriving remote team is who you let onto that team. And we know from a grow-ing body of research that just looking for star talent isn't all that successful unless they're also a great fit for your team. So pay special attention during the hiring process to each candidate's skills and past history with collaboration, communication, and self-motivation. And remember: remote work makes team-work *more* important, not less so. The people who work with new hires will have the biggest effect on their performance. So give them a say in who gets hired as well.

RULES FOR REMOTE LEADERS

There's a lot to consider when looking for new remote team-mates. Here's a quick review of our rules for remote-team leaders to keep top of mind when hiring:

- To ensure the new talent will thrive on your team, ask the following questions:
    * Are they collaborators?
    * Are they communicators?
    * Are they self-motivated?
- Skip the brainteasers.
- When onboarding, put connection over documentation.

And if you're looking for tools to help implement these rules for hiring and onboarding with your team, you can get several resources, like templates, worksheets, videos, and more, at davidburkus.com/resources.

4

BUILDING BONDS FROM AFAR

The idea of working on a remote team can seem lonely. In-person teammates are somewhat forced to interact with, and hence build connections with, the rest of their team. On a remote team, those organic interactions must be replaced by deliberate activities. If done well, they can actually build deeper bonds than when left to co-located chance.

SOCIAL MEDIA COMPANY Buffer does a lot of things differently. They are fully transparent, meaning their company financial information (including the salary of every employee) is available to everyone, whereas most companies default to secrecy. They are also fully remote, whereas most companies have only experimented with remote work (or had that experiment thrust upon them). But while there is a lot about the company that's different, there is one element when it comes to building a sense of culture and bonds between teammates that Buffer isn't contrarian about: meetups matter.

"While we wouldn't trade the value of being a distributed team, it's hard to deny the value of face time for team morale and serendipitous connections," said Stephanie Lee, Buffer's team experience manager. It's Lee's job to plan the company's annual retreat and product summit, as well as support each team in planning their annual meeting.

In the spring of every year, more than eighty "Bufferoos" get together for a week of connecting as a company and discussing high-level topics like vision and strategy. In the early days, these retreats were simply held at the company's infrequently used offices in San Francisco, but when the company went fully distributed, their retreat locations started moving all over the world, too. "We try to alternate between a North American location, a European location, and somewhere in a sort of Asia/APAC region," said Carolyn Kopprasch, Buffer's chief of special projects.

While the agenda for these retreats tends to focus on high-level matters, they also make sure to build in plenty of time for team meetings and bonding events. And it's during that in-person, unstructured time that bonds get built the most. Every Thursday of the Monday-through-Friday retreat is a complete day off, when individuals are given a "Buffer Fun Fund" to explore the surrounding area and enjoy activities together — everything from spa visits to skydiving. And every Friday ends with a gratitude session, where the entire company takes turns passing around the microphone and giving any employee an opportunity to express their appreciation to a team or an element of the company.

In addition to the annual retreat, Buffer also funds a smaller meeting for each team in the company. This gives teams a period of in-person work time, which helps them better understand how each teammate communicates and makes coordinating work easier during the rest of the year. "At a co-located company, you might call these off-sites," Lee explained. "For us, every day is an off-site, so these special gatherings are called 'on-sites!'" The on-sites are also one week long, but rather than focus on company-level issues, they give team leaders free rein to choose their objectives for the week. Some teams focus on goal setting or strategy, while others run "hackathons" where they specifically focus on improving some product or feature of a product. These on-sites aren't required, but most teams take advantage of the opportunity. And most teams deliberately schedule their on-sites about six months after the annual retreat, to maximize the bonding effect of the in-person meetings.

While it's certainly possible to build connections remotely, most remote teams have found that they accelerate their gains by taking a little bit of the money saved on office space and reallocating it to sharing physical space for a week or two every year.

Without a deliberate strategy in place to bring together a remote team physically and emotionally, remote work can be much more draining than it has to be. Loneliness is one of the emotions most frequently reported by those working from anywhere. And it can have a significantly negative effect on every teammate if not kept in check.

In looking at the research, loneliness at work has been found to reduce task performance, limit creative thinking, and impair reasoning and decision-making. Perhaps that's why researchers at the Gallup organization found that those with strong social connections at work were more engaged, produced higher-quality work, and called in sick less often. Outside of work, the effects of loneliness are even worse. In a 2010 meta-analysis, experiencing loneliness and having weak social connections was found to reduce a person's life span by the equivalent of smoking fifteen cigarettes a day or drinking more than six alcoholic beverages a day.

Clearly, building bonds between teammates matters. But building bonds on a virtual team is one of the hardest jobs remote leaders take on. Fortunately, there are some practical, evidence-based actions you can take to strengthen connections and decrease loneliness on your team.

In an 18-month study of remote workers, researchers found that the distant nature of teams was most often seen as a barrier to developing friendships with teammates. The researchers, led by management professor Beth Schinoff, conducted more than a hundred interviews with employees of a global technology company across an eighteen-month time frame and even observed a real-life "meetup" of those same employees. While remoteness was a barrier, remote-team members found ways around it and developed not only positive working relationships, but friendships as well.

The first step was to develop what the researchers called "cadence." They define cadence between team members as understanding who the other person is and predicting how they will interact with them. Cadence helps remote-team members coordinate when and how to collaborate. It develops more easily in in-person teams, partly because in-person teams often work the same hours. It's easy to develop cadence with someone when you just have to look up over your cubicle wall and start an information-rich, face-to-face conversation.

The researchers found that work-related cadence set the stage for nonwork bonds to form. Remote workers with cadence were more likely to talk about nonwork topics, connect on social media, or reach out for support after a personal setback. As leader of your remote team, you're in the best position to help your people build cadence with one another and eventually build bonds. Doing so is vital to your people's health and happiness and that of the company. In this chapter, we will look at tried-and-true ways to build connection virtually, and we'll take a deeper dive into the on-site that works so well for Buffer and would be a great exercise for any remote team.

Setting Your Team Up to Build Bonds

We've already touched on a few tips that will help your team start to build cadence through a shared understanding of everyone's unique situation. But to go further and begin to build bonds, you need to structure deliberately unstructured time for your people to chat — about both work and life. This might sound like a massive challenge, but there are actually a few relatively simple and inexpensive ways to achieve it. Here are a few to try.

Find time for *fika*. The Swedish tradition that translates simply as "to have coffee," *fika* is much more than just getting a warm drink. *Fika* is a ritual meetup between two people taking a break from work and socializing. The coffee is just the excuse to connect. Many remote companies have experimented with their own digital *fika*s and found them to be a vital tool for building connection. In the digital version, two people partner up to take a short break and chat about nonwork topics. It works best when the pairs are random, but leaders can also let people self-select while encouraging everyone to be deliberate about connecting with those with whom they don't chat often. Make sure these are scheduled during work hours so no one feels like it intrudes on their off-work time. And if you really want to encourage *fika*, ask a few people to share what they learned during the next team call. There's no set agenda for *fika*, but you can help seed the conversation by providing questions to ask each other during the break. Some of my favorites:

- What was your first job?
- Where is your favorite place to vacation?
- Who is your favorite superhero? Why?
- If you could teach a class, what would it be about?

In asking these questions, you don't have to go deep into each other's personal lives. You just want to keep the conversation going and keep teammates learning a little bit more about one another — and looking forward to the next *fika*.

Plan shared meals. Like *fika* but for the whole team. When in-person teams break for lunch or other meals, they bond over an activity that humans have shared for millennia. A 2017 study from Robin Dunbar (one of the world's leading researchers on communities and building bonds) found that people who eat socially are happier, are more engaged in the community, and have more friends. And a 2018 study showed that business-people who eat communal meals (traditional in Chinese and Indian cultures, less traditional in the West; we call it "family style") collaborate better and reach deals faster. You might not be able to re-create a communal, shared meal across a large circular table with your whole team, but you can add shared, virtual meals to everyone's calendar. The best example of this I've seen on remote teams is at the ten-person distributed company

Lawyerist, which holds regular Taco Tuesday lunches. Team members join a video call to share lunch together. Simulating the communal meal, teammates order tacos from their favorite local restaurant. It's completely optional to join, but anyone who shows up and shows their tacos gets the cost of the meal covered by the company.

Partner teammates for work sprints. While some people thrive working in isolation, others need to feel like they are not alone. Partnering for work sprints allows for a balance between the two options. In a work sprint, two (or more) people sign into a videoconference and, after exchanging a few hellos, settle into focusing on work. Their video stays on, but the application moves to the back of everyone's desktop while they focus on their work and work in silence. Breaks are scheduled at a designated stopping point, but not required. Not only does this provide a small opportunity to connect and engage, but decades of research have shown that people are motivated to work harder — in a variety of ways — when others are watching. Studies show people run faster, are more creative, and work harder on math problems when they know others are watching them. Even a creepy-looking pair of eyes to signal that their screen was being monitored led people to think they had worked harder. But I don't recommend installing any kind of spying software. The trick isn't to signal to employees that Big Brother is always watching, but to invite them to find a partner on the team to help keep them accountable, and vice versa. I even used this technique when writing this book, signing into a standing Zoom call with two author friends of mine. We wrote in twenty-five-minute sprints, chatted for five, and then did it again. I'm actually not sure you would be reading this now without those two faces in the upper right corner of my computer, motivating me to keep going. And there's another great side effect here. When you're trying to work in isolation, family members might not respect your boundaries. But if they think you're on a conference call, they're much more likely to leave you alone. (Just don't tell my kids.)

Hold office hours — and encourage others to do the same. If tactics like *fika* or work sprints feel too structured or inauthentic, encourage your team to set regular office hours when they're available for work-related or non-work-related discussion. You could do this as an open video call that's just left on for people to jump into, or an open block of time on the calendar for anyone to reserve. I was a full-time business school professor for almost a decade, and, unlike a lot of my peers, I found office hours to be one of the most effective meetings I was a part of — actually, I found it to be the only effective meeting I was a part of. All professors would post a regular schedule of times they were in their office and available for questions. But often one small question about the course would turn into a much larger discussion about school, life, future career plans, and a host of other topics that deepened the professor-student relationship. And if no one showed up, then I had a nice block of time to clear out my email inbox.

Host office scavenger hunts. We've covered how having team members give a virtual tour of their workspace helps to build shared expectations. Office scavenger hunts take that concept one step further and can be done on a regular basis (instead of only when a new teammate joins or someone changes workspaces). In this version, teammates are asked to look around their office and grab items that are personally meaningful to them. Once everyone returns, show-and-tell begins, each member taking a turn displaying what they grabbed. My favorite version of this is conducted with three items: something that makes you productive, something that makes you proud, and something that makes you laugh. You end up sharing tips on getting work done but also get a peek inside the personalities of the people on the other end of all those pixels.

Create team rituals. We're not talking about fire walking, long-distance quests, or even a new ice bucket challenge. But we are talking about a regular, specific action or group activity that is unique to your team. For as long as humans have formed tribes, they've used rituals to bond those tribes together. Most high-performing teams regularly engage in shared rituals because they create a sense of group identity and build trust. Your team should as well. These can be seriously meaningful rituals — one group I admire developed a set of core values and ac-

companying wristbands so that, before any meeting, participants reflect on the values and choose one wristband to wear
to signal to others their focus for the meeting. But they can also
be playful—another team holds a regular "talk" series where
different members come prepared with a five-minute lecture
on any topic that interests them. Rituals can even be combined
with other bonding elements in this section—Lawyerist's Taco
Tuesday is much more about the ritual than about the carnitas.

These six activities aren't the only ones you can facilitate,
but they are a great place to get started. Experiment with all
of them, modify them as you see fit, or ditch them entirely in
favor of something that feels like a better fit for your team. It's
up to the team to decide which activities become traditions.
But as your team grows and works together longer, you should
consider instituting one specific tradition: the on-site.

Meeting Up On-Site

As we already saw with Buffer, meeting in person and occu-
pying the same physical space is still one of the fastest ways to
build connection. So if you can, **plan on-sites.** Ideally, a company with remote teams is getting all its employees together
on a fairly regular basis. This is a great time to focus on high-
level strategy, goal setting, and other companywide initiatives,
while also providing ample time for socialization. But individ-

ual teams need time for smaller on-sites as well. These times can be used to discuss teamwide goals but could also be just an in-person, all-team work sprint where the team alternates between working together and breaking together.

However these might look, remote leaders should try to find time to get just their teams together for additional face time. The easiest way would be scheduling your team on-site around an industry conference. If the majority of the team would benefit from attending, surely they would benefit from connecting with one another after hours, too. And there's little added expense if the conference was already budgeted for. But if you can find additional budget, plan for a three-to-five-day dedicated meeting at a unique and memorable location.

As you approach the on-site, *over*-communicate the logistical details. Don't assume everyone has the same familiarity with travel logistics or the same comfort level being in new places. This is a lesson Lee and Kopprasch learned quickly at Buffer. When planning retreats or on-sites that required international travel, they found out that some teammates had never traveled internationally, didn't have passports, or had never been on an airplane before. If possible, set up a "frequently asked questions" shared document with your team and update it *any* time a new question about the meeting comes in. That way, you are going out of your way to make your team comfortable, but not adding too much additional work to your task list.

During the on-site, balance the agenda between making progress on team projects and making time to connect and bond as a team. This might be a half-and-half agenda for the day, or different themes for different days. You can take whatever liberties you want with the agenda, but be sure to have an agenda. Have a plan for how the time will be spent so you know it was spent well.

Lastly, if you can't bring the whole team together as often as you would like, make sure you're helping the team coordinate their own in-person visits whenever they happen to travel near each other. You don't need it to feel obligatory, but reach out to teammates for a quick visit (or in-person *fika*) if you know you're going to be in town. Gradually, other members of the team will do the same for one another.

Remote teams work well, but only if the team truly feels like a team. Individual remote workers struggle with feelings of loneliness and isolation, which are the nature of the work, but they don't have to be the nature of your team. If you take a few deliberate steps to build bonds between individual members of your team, and maybe even bring the team together physically, you'll find you have brought them much closer together emotionally — and more emotional bonds will quickly turn into more team wins.

RULES FOR REMOTE LEADERS

Building bonds between members of your remote team matters. Without a deliberate plan for connection, loneliness can creep up on anyone and drag their work and life down. Here's a quick review of our rules for remote-team leaders when building bonds on your team:

- Find time for *fika*.
- Plan shared meals.
- Partner teammates for work sprints.
- Hold office hours — and encourage others to do the same.
- Host office scavenger hunts.
- Create team rituals.
- Plan on-sites.

And if you're looking for tools to help build bonds on your team, you can get several resources, like templates, worksheets, videos, and more, at davidburkus.com/resources.

5

COMMUNICATING VIRTUALLY

When each member of your remote team is working in isolation, coordinating that work becomes even more important. Communicating virtually means setting the right expectations about what types of communication are used and how often. The goal is to be able to talk about the work being done and still leave enough time to actually do it.

B ASECAMP ISN'T JUST a company that embraces remote work. Basecamp was all but founded remotely. Accordingly, they hold some strong opinions on the role of communication in getting work done, because they've seen how powerful a tool communication can be — when implemented correctly.

Originally started as a web design agency, the company had what many consider its pivotal moment in 2001, when founder Jason Fried connected with programmer David Heinemeier

Hansson and hired him to create an application the company could use to manage projects. Fried was based in Chicago but didn't hesitate to hire Copenhagen-based Hansson once he believed Hansson was the right person for the job. They would just have to make the distance work. And they did. Their success with communication and coordination of work was instrumental not only in its pivot to becoming a product company, but in its becoming one of the premier tools for project management, especially among remote teams.

Pretty soon, the project management program Hansson had developed was being requested by their web design clients, who got a peek inside of the tool while collaborating on projects and wanted to use it to manage other projects inside their own companies. So the company started offering it as a product — and it quickly became more popular than any of their design services. So Fried decided to pivot to a software-as-a-service company, with Hansson as a partner and key player. They do have a Chicago office, but no one is expected to work there . . . or even live anywhere near Chicago. Only about a dozen or so people utilize the office on a regular basis. Fried has even designed it to resemble not so much a traditional office as a collection of remote-work spaces, with "library rules" for chitchat and sound panels hung everywhere to dampen even those small voices.

Together, Fried and Hansson even write books, give interviews, and deliver talks advocating for remote work. And in

2014, they sold off every other product in their portfolio to focus exclusively on marketing Basecamp. (And yes: Basecamp is
the name of the company *and* the name of the product.)

Fried and Hansson aren't just pro–remote teams; they're
downright anti-office. This is especially true when it comes to
how they see the office environment impacting communication. There is more communication in an in-person team, but
that's not necessarily a good thing. They describe the modern
office as an "interruption factory." In their 2013 book *Remote,* a
manifesto on the need for remote teams, they write that "a busy
office is like a food processor — it chops your day into tiny bits."
Between an endless stream of meetings, constant interruptions
from coworkers, and the nonstop pinging of email programs
(which often can't be adjusted because an IT worker somewhere decided to lock you out of the settings for your own
computer), the workday of the modern office employee looks a
lot like what comes out of a kitchen device in some late-night
infomercial ("it slices . . . it dices") and not like something that's
conducive to focused, deep work.

It may be surprising to learn that the first of Basecamp's core
guiding principles for internal communication is "You can
not not communicate." While Fried, Hansson, and the team at
Basecamp recognize that the office creates an environment of
constant, distracting interruptions, they also emphasize that
working remotely can't mean you work in a vacuum. Effective
communication is a vital component of getting work done —

the key is to learn efficient ways for communicating effectively about the projects you're working on without being distracted from actually working on them.

How do you strike that balance? Fried and Hansson would say your internal communication should be "real-time sometimes, asynchronous most of the time." In fact, that's the second rule of thumb in their internal communications guide, and that principle reveals a core underlying challenge with managing communication on remote teams.

It's not one problem. It's two problems.

Communication isn't just communication. It's asynchronous communication and synchronous communication. Just setting expectations for when to use each and creating some norms around each goes a long way toward closing the interruption factory . . . without leaving anyone out of the loop. Let's take a closer look at both types in order to understand how and when to use them to your team's advantage.

Asynchronous Communication

Inside the much larger category of asynchronous communication, there are a lot of types and tools to help keep people connected. Asynchronous can be email, message boards, comments on shared documents, or group chat. But whatever tool is chosen, one thing needs to be held to firmly: it needs to be truly asynchronous. Meaning the communication forum needs to be paired with an expectation that people *won't* respond immediately.

Why? Unless there's a decision to be made, communicating *about* work is rarely as productive as doing the work itself. One of the major benefits of remote teams is that the remote element theoretically provides individuals with long stretches of uninterrupted time to focus on tasks that actually create value. But if remote workers are expected to always be available for communication, that benefit quickly dissipates.

Consider what, for most of us, is the most constant part of our workday communication: email. In a 2012 study of office workers, researchers Gloria Mark and Stephen Voida, from the University of California, Irvine, found that participants who were blocked from the constant flow of email communication were more focused, more productive, and less stressed. Mark and Voida first allowed participants to work as normal during a three-day "baseline" period in which their workflow was observed through digital monitoring software that kept track of what computer programs workers were using and for how long. They also had their heart rates measured as a proxy for stress levels. Once the three days were complete, the researchers installed an email filter on participants' computers that would silence all incoming notifications and file away any new messages to a dedicated folder for later reading. This "no email" condition lasted for five days, during which time the participants still had their computer usage tracked and their heart rates monitored.

Without the constant distraction, all employees but one spent significantly more time in each computer program they used, which suggests that they were more focused on one task at a time. They also experienced much less stress than in their established baseline, despite being more productive. And their communication habits changed as well. Without back-and-forth email pings, participants were more likely to pick up the phone and have an information-rich conversation with their colleagues.

It wasn't the work that was stressing them out; it was constantly having to stop working so they could talk about the work they were just distracted from doing.

This study supports what has likely been a suspicion of employees who feel overwhelmed not just by the volume of messages in their inbox but by the number of inboxes and portals they have to check. Whether it's email or a more recent communication tool like Slack, asynchronous communication can backfire wildly if it's "always on" and employees are expected to respond quickly to each new message. In terms of which tools are the most interruptive, specifically, group chat applications have quickly displaced email as the biggest focus stealers.

Asking employees to keep a group chat window open is like demanding they attend an all-day meeting with no agenda where participants pop in and out at random and speak only in sentence fragments — all while you're expected to be accomplishing your daily work.

But, as the Mark-Voida study shows, abandoning a group chat platform and going back to email won't solve the problem if the same expectations are at play. Instead, the solution is to develop shared expectations and norms about frequency of communication and then *stick to those rules*. In most cases, a response within twenty-four hours is more than reasonable and should likely be the default expectation. If a faster response is needed, mention it in your request or consider moving the conversation to synchronous communication. Here are a few more guidelines to make asynchronous communication work for, and not against, your team:

Write clearly and concisely. There are a few technologies for sharing audio and video messages synchronously, but thus far they haven't been widely adopted. So, for the foreseeable future, text communication is going to be the dominant method of sharing information. (You already knew that, though . . . just look at your email inbox.) That means that being a great writer is a vital element of being a great teammate. Clear writing is clear thinking. It's also the best way to get your point across. Favor simple sentence structure. Keep language as concise as possible. Avoid jargon unless you know everyone in the discussion is familiar with the terms. Use active voice as much as possible (unless you're a lawyer deliberately trying to avoid culpability with passive-voice phrases like "mistakes were made").

Don't assume widespread consensus — or even acknowledgment. This applies even if something was said on the all-hands channel or sent out in a teamwide email. If you need consensus, ask for it. If you need confirmation of receipt, ask for it. And if you need either by a certain time or date, state that clearly. Depending on the situation, you could state that if you don't hear from people by a set deadline, you'll assume consensus then. Just don't assume it automatically. It may create a tad more work in the short term, counting replies from each team member, but it will save you a lot more work in the long term than if you barrel ahead on a project only to find a few days or weeks later what people's real objections are.

Infuse positivity into your writing. It's easy enough to misinterpret sarcasm or dry humor in messages from our spouses, partners, or close friends. It's almost a given that similar phrases shared with less familiar colleagues will be misread. And it's not necessarily the fault of the writer. Research shows that recipients of written media like email or text chat are more likely to suffer from a "negativity effect," meaning the lack of emotional cues misleads readers to interpret the messages as significantly more negative than the writer intended. Don't sacrifice a written tone that's warm and personable for something more businesslike unless the situation (or team of lawyers) calls for it.

At the same time, **assume a positive intent** when reading messages from others. They may not have read this book (or not yet; you could always send them a copy) and they may not be aware that their "just the facts" communication is coming off as cold and calculated. So warm it up for them as you read it, and when in doubt, assume the best.

In a remote-team environment, asynchronous communication — done well — should be the default mode of communication. Not just because it spares everyone's calendar from too many meetings and too little real work but also because it respects the varied work schedules those calendars are structured around. Still, there are times when an email, chat, or message board discussion isn't sufficient. In those cases, we should pivot to synchronous communication, which requires its own set of norms and expectations in order to be effective.

Synchronous Communication

When we look at situations where synchronous or real-time conversations are called for, it's tempting to assume that our cutting-edge technologies have made these discussions dramatically better. With modern technology, you can run a one-hundred-person digital meeting where everyone can see each other's faces against virtual backdrops while also keeping one eye on a running stream of group chat and private messages, all while trying to remember whether or not they're on mute.

When you put it that way, it doesn't sound all that conducive to communication.

A growing body of research reinforces that videoconferences aren't that big an improvement for communication. Our assumption is that they should be. We've all heard the (now debunked) statistic that 93 percent of communication is nonverbal, and video calls let us bring that factor back to the conversation. But it turns out we're much better listeners when we tune some of those nonverbals out.

In a series of studies conducted on communication, researcher Michael Kraus found that voice-only communication elicited the highest rate of empathic accuracy—the ability to gauge the emotions, thoughts, and feelings of other individuals. In one experiment, Kraus paired up nearly three hundred participants for a conversation with a total stranger. Half of the pairs conducted that conversation in a well-lit room; the other half had the same conversation, but in a pitch-black room. Afterwards, all participants were given surveys designed to rate their emotions and the perceived emotions of their partners. In collecting the results, Kraus found that participants in the pitch-black room were more likely to judge the emotions felt by their partner accurately.

In a follow-up experiment, Kraus designed interactions that mimic many workplace conversations. As in the first experiment, participants were paired together for a discussion. This time, two interactions between each pair were conducted through a videoconferencing platform. In the first, participants used the voice-only feature to conduct the call. In the second, they turned the camera on for voice and video. Afterwards, a similar assessment of their and their partners' emotions were given to all participants. Just as with the first experiment, participants were better able to accurately gauge the emotions of their partner in the voice-only condition. Kraus's research is in line with broader research showing that vocal cues are more critical to accurately judging emotions than facial expressions.

The eyes aren't the window to the soul; the voice box is.

As everyone who's been employed longer than a day has likely experienced, emotions run high during workplace discussions. And the ability to accurately read the emotions *behind* what's being said is a crucial skill. So it's surprising to find that ditching endless video calls and using "old school" technologies like a phone call might actually achieve more communication in less time. But the evidence supports it.

And beyond just enhancing our ability to process what the other person is saying, old-fashioned audio-only phone calls are likely to be shorter in duration than video calls, letting each person on the call get back to doing real work faster. So when you've got an issue that asynchronous or text communication can't solve, reach for the phone before you reach for a calendar invite to a video call. Seven minutes on the phone will beat out both an entire day spent emailing back and forth *and* an hour-long videoconference.

So: **Voice first, video later.**

Check yourself before going on camera. There will still be situations where you need to move from voice to video. Especially if multiple people are involved and reading the cues on who would like to speak works better if you can see everyone. So in those cases, remember that when you are on camera with someone, *you are on camera* with someone. That means check your appearance before switching your camera on, at least from the waist up. A remote-work world means we're all a little more relaxed about dress code. But if you look like you just got out of bed, people will assume that you . . . just got out of bed. And put some thought into your background. In a 2020 survey conducted in the midst of COVID-19 lockdowns, people definitively preferred seeing the real room behind the video callers, not a fake picture of a Hawaiian sunset.

Put a lighting source behind the camera. You might have a great view out the window behind you, but people on a video call with you won't see it. Instead, as the camera struggles to adjust its settings, you'll be a silhouette against a square blur of light. If you're not an anonymous whistleblower in some investigative documentary, show us your face.

Know how to make eye contact. And this is a pro tip from someone who's filmed a *lot* of video and led a *lot* of webinars: Don't make eye contact; make camera lens contact. Making eye contact with a person's face on the screen usually makes it look like you're staring at their chin or at your computer screen.

When you're speaking, look straight at the lens of your camera. You could even draw a smiley face on a sticky note and tape it next to your camera lens to remember to look up and smile. For webinars, I use a passport photo of my wife taped next to my webcam. The photo was rejected by the State Department because she was smiling . . . but now I can't help but smile every time I see it.

So look at the camera, not at the person, and you'll look like you're looking at the person, not the camera. Got it?

And while "voice first, video later" is a good rule to follow, it bears remembering that it should really be "work first, voice second, video later." Modern communications technology is absolutely amazing, but it's also too tempting. Resist the urge to jump on a call or videoconference with someone every time you want to communicate something. Actively remind yourself that uninterrupted work is one of the core benefits of working remotely. Filling your people's days with calls works against that benefit. So, before picking up the phone, try to reflect on whether that phone call or allowing your people to continue to work without interruption would be more valuable.

Do You Need a Virtual Water Cooler?

Setting expectations and norms for communication will have a drastically positive impact on your team's productivity. When asynchronous communication is the norm and synchronous communication is kept to a minimum, your team members have much more autonomy over their schedules than an office-based team would. But there's one thing many teams have found an office provides that can be an overlooked opportunity for important communication: the water cooler.

Everyone needs mindless breaks throughout the day. The chitchat that used to happen at the water cooler or the office kitchen area was a good way to reset one's mind and quickly connect with coworkers over nonwork chat. So many remote teams, and wholly remote companies, have sought to re-create that virtual water cooler with a team chat room that's always available for people to drop in and out of as they please.

I know. I know.

We just stressed the importance of *not* having a group chat window always open. This is where good leadership comes into play. The goal isn't to be constantly connected. At the same time, many teams have benefited from having a place to take some natural breaks, chat about what television shows they're bingeing, and share a few photos or videos of family, friends, or funny felines. And a good amount of research suggests that making room for "small talk" and other nonwork conversation really does increase individual performance — so long as it's not a constant distraction.

So the key seems to be that each team member should feel their presence is never required but always welcome. The control still rests with each individual. You've just provided a place for them to have nonwork chats that help keep the team connected.

And do ensure that this is a place for nonwork discussions . . . Otherwise it just devolves into one more place team members feel they have to check regularly in order to get their work done.

Communication is the oxygen of any relationship, and that's especially true for remote teams. Each team member may be working in isolation, but choreographing that work requires deliberate communication. Without those deliberate guidelines, teammates can fall into the trap of going off on fruitless tangents or find themselves repeating the work of someone else on the team. Every great remote team has clear norms and expectations for what, when, how, and how often they communicate. And now your remote team has them, too.

RULES FOR REMOTE LEADERS

We covered a lot in this chapter on communication, including when and how to be asynchronous and synchronous with your team. Here's a quick review of our rules for remote-team leaders:

- Asynchronous communication is the rule; synchronous is the exception.
- Write clearly and concisely.
- Don't assume consensus.
- Infuse positivity into your writing.
- Assume a positive intent.
- Voice first, video later.
- Check yourself before going on camera.
- Put a lighting source behind the camera.
- Know how to make eye contact.
- Provide a virtual water cooler.

And if you're looking for tools to help your team communicate virtually, you can get several resources, like templates, worksheets, videos, and more, at davidburkus.com/resources.

6

RUNNING VIRTUAL MEETINGS

As we learned in looking more closely at how the best remote teams communicate, virtual meetings are one of the few times when the entire team gets together at the same time. Done well, they can be an exciting opportunity to build connection between your people and give them greater clarity on the tasks at hand. Done poorly, they can be as loathed as . . . well . . . in-person meetings.

WOLFRAM RESEARCH MAY not be the largest remote company, but it's likely the oldest one still in business and still one of the most forward-thinking — and successful — when it comes to virtual meetings. At the very least, its CEO, Stephen Wolfram, is a founding father of the remote-work world, having started the company in 1987. He had relocated to start a research center at the University of Illinois at Urbana-Champaign and was looking to bring to market a product from his research. The university was (and still is) an under-rated center for computing minds, and Wolfram was able to find talented people quickly at the start. But eventually Champaign's talent pool just wasn't large enough. Wolfram wanted to be able to recruit from all over the world and didn't see a reason not to. The technology was there in 1987 to collaborate remotely. Why not use it?

So the company started hiring remote employees. And since it kept working, they kept using a remote strategy to find top talent — all the way to the eight hundred or so employees they have today. In fact, Wolfram decided to go remote himself and work from home or wherever he'd decided to travel to. "I've been a remote CEO since 1991," he boasts regularly.

The company is most known for its flagship product, WolframAlpha, an "answer engine" powered by artificial intelligence, curated data sources, and the company's own algorithms. If you've done a search on Microsoft's Bing or DuckDuckGo or if you've ever asked Siri or Alexa a question, odds are those programs tapped into WolframAlpha's system to bring you back an answer. In addition to opening up a world of answers to everyday users, Wolfram Research is also known inside its industry for opening up its company meetings for the world to watch (and sometimes participate in).

That's right. Wolfram Research livestreams its corporate meetings.

And what's even crazier: hundreds of people watch. Wolfram

has even amassed seven thousand followers on Twitch, a live-stream platform reserved almost exclusively for video gamers.

It started back in 2017. Being a remote company, it held its meetings almost entirely virtually. Instead of a typical grid of tiny, pixelated faces on a screen, most of the company's virtual meetings were held audio-only, with screen sharing. They were usually working on code or some other design element, so why not all be looking at that code on one device? "As much as possible, the goal in our meetings is to finish things," Wolfram explained. "To consult in with all the people who have input we need, and to get all the ideas and issues about something resolved." Screen sharing just seemed like the easiest way to do it.

As for livestreaming, Wolfram had been using the technology to increase transparency in the company for a long time. When WolframAlpha launched in 2009, the company live-streamed the process of taking the website live. Afterwards, they kept livestreaming software demos, and sometimes Wolfram would even casually open up a livestream whenever he was writing code. He'd developed a decent following online through those livestreams. "But I've always thought our internal design review meetings are pretty interesting, so I thought 'why not let other people listen in on them too?'" So, he did, and has been for over three years.

A typical meeting has anywhere from two to twenty people from inside the company on the line. If Wolfram is in the meeting, he'll make a brief introduction for the people watching the feed and then the meeting proceeds as usual. Except that the people watching often make themselves known via the text chat that runs alongside the broadcast. It's often questions for the team or a general discussion, but it can turn into comments or suggestions on what is being discussed. "It's like having instant advisors, or an instant focus group, giving us real-time input or feedback about our decisions," Wolfram reflected. "In fact, in most meetings at least one or two good ideas come from our viewers, that we're instantly able to incorporate into our thinking."

Livestreaming every company meeting sounds terrifying, but for Wolfram and his team it's been an astounding success. For everyone else, running meetings remotely is usually one of leaders' biggest fears. And their meetings aren't even broadcast for the world to see. In fact, "Virtual meetings don't work" is the most common response I hear when speaking to leaders at all levels about remote teams.

But let's be fair: in-person meetings rarely ever worked, either.

There's an entire research field of "meeting science" developing to study the effectiveness of organizational meetings, and the initial findings aren't good. In one study, researchers from the United States and the United Kingdom conducted an international survey of more than a thousand employees at all levels of organizations to get their perception of how effective their meetings really were. The vast majority of respondents' comments on meetings were negative. They cited poor planning, lack of an agenda, and other structural elements of the scheduled gathering people had to suffer through. The few comments that were positive primarily referred to the reasons *for* the meeting, like solving problems or helping shape culture. It's clear that meetings aren't going away any time soon — people see the value in holding them. It's in the execution of the meeting that all that value seems to disappear.

In a virtual meeting, these positives and potential negatives are heightened. It might be the only time this week or month that you get your entire team together at the same time, and it's your best chance for making sure people feel like they're part of a real team. At the same time, if their feelings after every meeting are "This whole thing could have been an email," that's going to shape their feelings about the overall team as well.

In addition, how many meetings you're asking people to attend will have a big effect on their perception of each meeting's effectiveness. In a 2019 study from Owl Labs on the state of remote work, remote workers reported attending more meetings each week than in-person workers did. And 14 percent of remote workers said they were attending more than ten meetings per week. That's a lot of meetings. And a lot of them probably stem from the faulty assumption that meetings are the best mode of communication for a team. But remember from the last chapter that face-to-face, group communication should be the medium of last resort so that every time you do meet, your team is more likely to find the meeting effective — because it *is* more likely to be effective.

So, in this chapter, we'll offer a step-by-step guide to planning and executing an effective virtual meeting. And we'll offer some tips to keep top of mind while you're hosting the session as well. Planning the meeting right, running it right, and following up right are keys to making sure your people feel like they're on the right remote team with the right leader. You.

How to Run an Effective Virtual Meeting, in Eight Easy Steps

Whether it's your first virtual meeting with your team or your forty-seventh weekly meeting, here are the steps to follow to make it the best one ever.

1. **Plan with purpose.** "It's time for our regularly scheduled meeting" isn't a good enough reason. The reason *can* be that every once in a while, you want to connect everyone together. But even then, you'll want to declare that up front. It will make the planning process much easier, since people will have realistic expectations about what will be discussed and can plan accordingly. Other solid reasons for the meeting are to deliberate on an issue, to generate ideas, to make a decision, or to collaborate real-time on a document. Keep it to one purpose per meeting. Any more and you should consider breaking it up

into two smaller meetings (even if both happen on the same day).

2. **Pick the right invitees, and only the right ones.** Not everyone on your team needs to be at every meeting, and every event invite you send is a distraction from the real work they want to do. Remember that the cost of a one-hour meeting with nine people isn't one hour; it's nine hours. And as the number of people in a meeting increases, the effectiveness of the meeting generally plummets. So be a smart spender of your people's time and keep the guest list as short as possible.

3. **Build the right agenda.** You should have an agenda for every meeting, but it should be the right agenda. Research has shown that just having an agenda doesn't enhance anyone's perception of the meeting's effectiveness. What matters is what's in the plan and how well the meeting sticks to the plan. Instead of using generic titles, use questions. So "Marketing Issues" becomes "How might we get the same return on a decreased advertising budget?" and "Miscellaneous Items" becomes "What vital information do we have to share with each other?" Questions have two benefits. First, they put people in the right frame of mind when you send out the agenda (and you absolutely should send it out ahead of time). Second, they help everyone know if the meeting was indeed effective. If we got our questions answered, it was indeed an effective meeting.

4. **Open the line ten minutes early.** Every meeting should start on time. But if you think about the dynamics of in-per-

son meetings, there's often a pre-meeting phase that allows for valuable team bonding. Maybe it's because they walk to the meeting together or maybe it's because they got to the room early to chat. In a virtual setting, if you start the meeting right on time, you're depriving the team of that socialization phase. So open up the call ten minutes early and let people casually enter in (and tell your team you'll be doing so). You can even facilitate this stage with a few questions planned to help people share what's going on in their world. (And if you're starting ten minutes early, make sure that *you* sign onto the conference platform five to ten minutes earlier than that. You don't want to be troubleshooting technology issues while your teammates are sharing about their baby's first steps or their recent vacation.)

5. **Capture minutes.** You don't need every meeting to adhere to Robert's Rules of Order. But you should have a scribe (other than the facilitator) assigned to keep track of what was said. In particular, you want to make sure you're documenting unforeseen issues, new ideas, and any action items that come from decisions. The exact time stamps of who said what and when don't matter as much as making sure we know what ideas were presented and who committed to take what action on them.

6. **Stay on topic.** As the meeting progresses, make sure you're staying on topic and sticking to your planned allotments of time. Oversharers who dominate the conversation can get you off track quickly if you're not diligent, and so can those

problem-askers who pretend to ask questions but really just want to put their long, drawn-out statements out there anytime you call for questions. You built the agenda with purpose, so it's there to take the blame if you have to interrupt and ask them to table their thoughts for offline time. And if someone arrives late, you don't need to waste time catching them up. They have the agenda, and they can always watch the recording or read the meeting minutes afterwards.

7. **Close with a review.** As the meeting time draws to a close, bring everyone back together with a quick review of what just happened. Have the appointed scribe review the minutes if needed; otherwise just run through the questions that made up the agenda items and check that everyone feels those questions were answered. Finally, confirm that action items are understood by the assigned person and, if possible, get a time commitment for each action.

8. **Leave the line open.** Call the meeting to a close at or before the planned time, but don't feel the need to shut down the call right away. Just as you opened the call a few minutes early, leave it open for folks to continue socializing afterwards. If you're the "host" of the conference call, that might mean you have to stay until everyone else is signed off, but you should be able to mute the audio and disable your video if you need to focus on other tasks.

Afterwards, be sure to send out the minutes from the meeting and let people know where they can watch/listen to any recordings if they missed it. When you do, you'll likely get a few pieces of feedback from members of your team that'll help you adapt the meeting flow to their liking and make the next one ever better.

A Few Tips to Make Virtual Meetings Even Better

If you follow the above steps, your virtual meetings will likely be seen as valuable before they start *and* will still be seen that way long after you've completed them. But there are a few more things to keep in mind when you're planning and facilitating virtual meetings.

Share the pain. If you're leading a global team, or even one that's just scattered across a continent or two, then time zones become a big factor. If you're always scheduling meetings at times convenient to you (or even convenient to the greatest number of people), then you're sending the message that those who have to sign on at inconvenient times are less vital to the team or less worthy of consideration. So share the pain of bad meeting times, rotating them regularly so that everyone gets a few good times and a few bad ones, but *everyone* feels connected and vital to the team.

Everyone on video; or no one. In the same vein as sharing the pain, default to a virtual meeting if even one of your teammates can't make an in-person meeting. If anyone has to call in, then everyone should. Mixing a few people in the room together and a few others as talking heads on a digital screen gives too much power to those in the room and can potentially shut down vital contributions from those who feel they're second-class meeting citizens. In addition, if everyone's calling into a videoconference, make sure they've got video turned on, unless there's a *very* good and temporary reason not to be. And I know we talked about how voice-only communication is great for one-on-one conversations, but in a meeting, we use a lot of visual cues to coordinate discussion and sense the overall emotion levels of the group. If someone can't be on video with the rest of the team for the entire meeting, then they likely can't focus on the meeting itself anyway. So go back to the first tip and make sure you've found the right time for the meeting.

Minimize presentation time. There's certainly value in taking some time on a virtual meeting to present new information or get everyone on the same page. But don't overdo the presentation time. The real magic of any meeting happens during discussion, but that's especially true for virtual meetings. Spending too much time having to listen to one person makes it more likely that teammates will casually minimize the meetings and click over to get some real work done or check their social media profiles. So even when someone is presenting, encourage pauses for questions and brief discussions every so often to re-engage people.

Use names often and encourage others to do the same. Speaking of reengagement, nothing is more attention-getting than hearing our own name. It helps draw in those who haven't yet contributed to the conversation and make them feel valued. Likewise, create a norm that everyone should identify themselves by name before speaking ("This is David. What if we . . ."). It helps create a sense of presence for the speaker and clarity for the listeners. It also makes it easier to find who's talking in the grid of tiny faces.

Start positive. Like most experiences, meetings are subject to a primacy effect — things mentioned in the beginning are more likely to be remembered. (You still remember "Share the pain," right? It was the first item on this list.) And that includes perceptions and emotions. So start positive and it will be remembered as a positive meeting. In fact, there's even some research suggesting that meetings have a contagion effect as well — which means that if a team leader starts off with positive energy, that energy and emotion will spread to the rest of the team as time progresses.

Break it up. Videoconferences can be draining. For a few different reasons, the primary one being that "Zoom fatigue" is a very real phenomenon. Our brains were not designed to be exposed to large faces or grids of tiny faces for very long without tiring, or worse. A study led by Stanford's Jeremy Bailenson found that videoconferences mess with our sense of personal space and can even trigger a panicked reaction. In a video call, our sense of how much someone is in our personal space is largely determined by how big the faces onscreen are. A large face feels like someone is up close and personal, and even triggered a fight-or-flight-like response in participants. And a series of small faces looks like a faraway crowd — all staring at the same person. Either situation isn't all that comfortable to our primitive, pre-Zoom brains. So for long meetings, providing frequent breaks to stretch your legs (and rest your eyes) goes a long way to reducing Zoom fatigue, as does breaking up what's onscreen between faces, slide decks, and other visuals that let the mind reset.

Break it out. If your team is too large and they're all on the call, consider planning for times when you break into smaller virtual rooms. It can increase the engagement of each person and keep oversharers from dominating the conversation. Just make sure you've got a plan to capture the great ideas that happened in each room and bring them back to the main discussion.

Keep a chat box open. Ideally, side discussions and running commentary are kept to a minimum so that attendees are focused on the main meeting. But there are always times when someone needs to send the facilitator a quick message, share a quick resource, or explain why they had to sign off unexpectedly. And when that happens, it's better for that to get captured in the chat window than to derail the entire discussion.

· · ·

Pair these tips with the steps for planning virtual team meetings and you'll be much more likely to tap into the brain power of everyone on the team — and keep them from feeling like you should have just sent an email. Virtual meetings run well are your best opportunity to get the entire team talking and facilitate a real sense of cohesion and collaboration among colleagues, no matter their distance.

RULES FOR REMOTE LEADERS

We covered a lot in this chapter on planning and running a highly effective virtual team meeting. Here's a quick review of our rules for remote-team leaders:

How to Run an Effective Virtual Meeting, in Eight Easy Steps:

1. Plan with purpose.
2. Pick the right invitees, and only the right ones.
3. Build the right agenda.
4. Open the line ten minutes early.
5. Capture minutes.
6. Stay on topic (and nip overtalking in the bud).
7. Close with a review.
8. Leave the line open.

A Few Tips to Make Virtual Meetings Even Better:

- Share the pain.
- Everyone on video; or no one.
- Minimize presentation time.
- Use names often and encourage others to do the same.
- Start positive.
- Break it up.

- Break it out.
- Keep a chat box open.

And if you're looking for tools to help implement these rules for running the best virtual team meetings, you can get several resources, like templates, worksheets, videos, and more, at davidburkus.com/resources.

7

THINKING CREATIVELY

Creative thinking has long been thought of as a solo endeavor. And in a remote environment, it might be even more tempting to believe that myth. But creativity works best when it works in teams and when it's not just a "brainstorming" meeting but a deliberate problem-solving process. You don't have to lose out on this process when your teammates are spread out in various locations — in fact, some of the best creative thinking can be done in remote teams.

O KAY, HOUSTON, WE'VE had a problem here."
Those were the troubling words of astronaut Jack Swigert, spoken just nine minutes after the crew of the Apollo 13 had ended a live broadcast in which they'd given the public a tour of the floating spacecraft and then wished them all good night. The crew had heard a short bang and felt a vibration and radioed the message down to mission control. A few minutes

later, commander Jim Lovell looked out the window and noticed a gas venting out of one of the craft's hatches. It was oxygen. A tank had exploded and was quickly leaking the precious
gas into the vacuum of space.

Thus began one of the most famous acts of problem-solving
on a remote team in human history. A crew of three astronauts
collaborating through radio signals with dozens of their teammates on the ground struggled to develop a plan that would
bring the three men home safely. A few hours later, after making the obvious call to abort any attempt to land on the moon,
the astronauts moved from the central command module to
the smaller lunar module. The command module ran on fuel
cells, which required the oxygen tank to power them. The lunar module, on the other hand, ran on batteries and, with a few
adjustments, it had enough power to last through the newly
improvised return trip. It had enough oxygen as well.

But one thing it didn't have was a way to remove all the
newly produced carbon dioxide that three men in a lunar
model for ninety-six hours would produce — the lunar module's carbon scrubbers had been designed for two men over a
thirty-six-hour period. Carbon dioxide is technically nontoxic,
but since it's heavier than air, it can displace it, meaning that in
an enclosed environment humans would begin getting less oxygen with every breath and eventually asphyxiate. No problem,
though: the-powered down command module had additional
carbon scrubbers and filters. They could just bring those over.

Not so fast.

It turned out the carbon scrubbers in the lunar module were circular, but the ones in the command module were square, and so were the filters. The astronauts and mission control were going to have to find a way to put a square filter into a round hole. In a remarkably short period of time, the crew on the ground figured out how to put an improvised adapter onto the lunar module's carbon scrubber using only parts available to the astronauts. And they got creative. The supplies list they radioed up to the astronauts included parts from their space suits, extra socks, and the cardboard cover of the crew's flight manual. The procedure checklist included steps like "Stuff the sock into the ventration hole in the center of the square scrubber."

But it worked.

The astronauts followed the nineteen-step checklist beautifully, and the "mailbox" (as they called the device) held together long enough for the crew to slingshot around the moon, climb back into the command module, and jettison their lifeboat lunar module just before reentering the atmosphere and splashing down in the Pacific Ocean — a little worse for wear, but alive, thanks to some incredible remote problem-solving.

Hopefully, in your life as a leader, you won't be asked to remotely solve such a high-stakes problem, but all leaders will be called upon to help their teams think creatively and solve problems collaboratively. When that happens, it might be tempting to long for the days of gathering everyone into a conference room, grabbing a whiteboard marker, and spitting out ideas as fast as you can. But, like the astronauts on the Apollo 13 mission, remote leaders don't have an in-person working space to solve problems. And, more important, the conference room approach to creative thinking might not have been all that effective anyway.

As I wrote in my first book, *The Myths of Creativity*, "creativity is a team sport." So in this chapter we'll cover not only the optimal procedure for getting your team to think creatively, but also when that thinking requires you to get the whole team together, and when it doesn't. And we'll share some best practices for bringing out your people's best ideas and making sure everyone's ideas get heard.

Can You Brainstorm on a Video Call?

That's probably the question I get most often when it comes to creative thinking in teams. One of the first reactions most leaders have when facing a problem they can't solve by themselves is to gather their people and kick off their tried-and-not-always-so-true method: brainstorming. We're trained in corporate America to equate any and all creative thinking with a brainstorming meeting. Get everybody in a room for an hour or so and generate as many ideas as we can.

But when you study the methods of some of the world's

most prolifically creative companies (and when you examine the research on creative thinking), you discover something pretty quickly. Creative thinking isn't a meeting; it's a process. Brainstorming, or any other method of rapid idea generation, is a part of that process, but it's not the entire process. In fact, the real work begins many steps beforehand.

So can you brainstorm on a video call? Yes. But that shouldn't be all you do. In fact, a brainstorming meeting shouldn't even be the only meeting you have when working on a problem. When looking at the creative problem-solving process and the limitations (and strengths) of remote teams, you probably need at least three different meetings at three points in the process.

Research suggests that the best decisions are made when you break up meetings into smaller meetings held separately. In a classic study in social psychology, researchers recruited participants for a decision-making meeting with a twist. After the groups had come to a decision, the researchers told participants to hold the meeting again, and make a decision again. The groups were not given any feedback on their first decision or given any instructions about needing to come to a different decision than they had in the first meeting. But most of the groups did. Moreover, the second decision was typically much more inclusive of ideas discussed and more creative overall than the first decision reached. One possible explanation for this is a quirk of human behavior to chase consensus. When we're in meetings, we tend to rally too quickly around the first idea that seems to gain momentum — partly because we want to get everyone to agree and partly because we just want to get out of the meeting. Meeting participants sacrifice genuine debate and deliberation for quick consensus. Breaking up a large meeting into several smaller ones with different goals helps prevent that harmful tradeoff.

So when you need to think creatively with your team to solve a problem, don't schedule one long meeting. Schedule three over the course of several days: a problem meeting, an idea meeting, and a decision meeting.

Start with a problem meeting. The purpose of the problem meeting is exactly what it sounds like: to discuss the problem. Often when we first encounter a situation, we're actually looking at the symptom of a different, underlying problem. The goal of this first meeting should be to step back and determine what problem, if solved, will have the most benefit. In doing so, we are looking to recruit as many people who might know something about the issue as we can and making sure they are given time to share their perspective. Tactics or methods like Sakichi Toyoda's "Five Whys" method or Kaoru Ishikawa's fishbone diagram can be useful here. (If you're unfamiliar with either, they are well worth a quick internet search.) But what's most important is that this meeting stay focused on discussing potential causes of the problem, as well as constraints. Yes: constraints. While we might associate creative thinking with boundless ideas and wandering minds, there's a wealth of research suggesting that constraints actually enhance our creativity. Moreover, constraints will provide the criteria by which solutions will later be judged. Instead of thinking "outside of the box," you want to use this meeting to decide which box to think inside of. The best version of that box is a simple question: "How might we _____?" The blank is the root problem you've discovered. Such as "How might we increase sales without increasing marketing expenses?" or "How might we reduce miscommunication across departments?" Asking an open-ended question reminds people that multiple possibilities exist — our job isn't to find the "right" answer, it's to find all of them and then choose the best one.

Then call an idea meeting. Once the problem is explored and the question written, we can call for the idea meeting. This is the meeting that most resembles brainstorming (and we have some tips for how to facilitate this meeting in the next section). But before you start spouting ideas, make sure you've got the right people in this virtual room as well. Depending on the problem, this may or may not be the same attendee list as at the problem meeting. In the problem meeting, we asked, "Who knows something about this issue?" But now, we also need to make sure we're including a much more diverse group of participants. In addition to adding new attendees because you've discovered the root cause and noticed it affects more people than you first thought, you'll also want to ask, "Who is typically excluded from these conversations?" and invite anyone who is often excluded for the wrong reasons (wrong title, too low on the organizational chart, too new to the company, or a host of other faulty assumptions). Once it's time for the meeting, open with a brief round of introductions. If you have the right attendee list, it's almost guaranteed that you'll have people from different teams on the call. So make sure everyone is familiar with the background and relevant experience of everyone else. Then briefly outline the problem you discovered, its constraints, the problem question ("How might we _____?"), and the ground rules for discussion. Depending on your team and the problem, those ground rules might change. But at a minimum you should have guidelines in place that encourage everyone to speak up, to minimize distractions, and to keep any criticisms focused on ideas. The goal of the idea meeting isn't to arrive at a final solution (that's what the next meeting is for). But once you've got a large list of ideas, it might be worth spending some time narrowing down or combining options to make the decision meeting easier and better.

End with a decision meeting. The final meeting, the decision meeting, doesn't need to be a separate meeting held on a different day—unless, of course, the attendee lists would change dramatically between the two meetings. But there should be some kind of break (bio-break, lunch break, nature break) between the idea meeting and this. Doing so provides the mental reset needed to avoid rallying around whatever ideas might have gained momentum during the idea meeting and provides everyone with a fresh perspective on the list of available options. In addition, taking even a short break provides many people with the opportunity to excuse themselves if they were part of the idea meeting but don't need to be around for the decision itself. Rather than jumping right into the list of ideas, start the decision meeting by reviewing the problem question and the constraints or any other criteria that will be used to judge an idea's merit. If there's a large list of options, consider an initial round of voting just to eliminate ideas that don't meet the criteria — but avoid using that voting round as a way to "rank" the remaining ideas. If the list isn't too large, then move right into discussing each idea in turn. Don't just talk about the strengths and weaknesses of the idea, but make sure everyone considers what the process of implementing the idea looks like as well. My favorite question to ask of each idea is "What would have to be true for this idea to work?" That way I'm sure everyone considers the environment around them when deciding on an idea's novelty and usefulness.

Often, by the time each idea is discussed in turn, the group has already found that one option or combination of options stands out. If not, that's okay. Continue the discussion with the goal of continuing to eliminate ideas. If you can't reach consensus, that's okay too. In fact, it's often a better idea to seek commitment rather than consensus. If a few people still disagree with a decision when it's made, that's a good sign that you've actually examined all relevant issues. If they don't, it's possible the consensus is actually the result of a blind spot or echo chamber effect and not reflective of the brilliance of the idea. But you do need to know that everyone who is affected by the decision leaves the meeting feeling heard and willing to implement the idea (even if it still wasn't their first choice).

Taken together, these three meetings ensure you've fully examined a problem, generated multiple solutions, and arrived at one of the best possible outcomes. It might seem like a logistical hassle to schedule three meetings with three different attendee lists. It does take more initial work than just jumping on a video call and spitballing ideas. But in the long term, it will likely save lots of time and effort — since the most likely idea generated in those singular meetings is "We need to discuss this further; let's schedule a follow-up meeting."

Facilitation Matters When Generating Ideas

Taking the time to deliberately plan out problem-solving meetings will go a long way toward making sure your team is thinking most creatively. But next to the right process, the right facilitator becomes a crucial element of any creative thinking process. As the team leader, you're likely the default choice for meeting facilitator. But if not, you'll want to make sure the right person is briefed on how to run the meeting most efficiently. Toward that end, here are a few things to remember when running any one of the three meetings discussed above:

Open with a warm-up. Specifically, for the idea meeting, it's best to begin the meeting with a quick warm-up activity to get everyone ready to generate ideas fast and furiously. There may be a "creativity muscle" that needs to be warmed up — but probably not. More important, a warm-up activity helps the group get comfortable with one another and with respecting and responding to ideas. This helps create the psychological safety needed to keep people from self-censoring their ideas. I've used a variety of warm-up activities in the past, from generating random uses of common objects, to generating deliberately wrong answers to common questions, to asking everyone to share their favorite "meeting fail." You don't need to spend too much time on the warm-up, but any time you do spend you'll likely earn back later when real ideas start flowing faster.

Cameras on, mute off, notifications off. If everything goes properly, these meetings will be lively. In an in-person setting, we rely on lots of visual cues to make sure we're not interrupting others and also to signal to the group that we would like to speak. In a virtual setting, these cues are harder to spot. If one or two members keep their cameras off and themselves muted, it's almost impossible. So, at the very least, during discussion portions, make sure everyone can see and hear everyone else. And encourage them to turn off any notifications on their computer that might cause a distraction. To the same end, make sure you've turned off any of the default notifications that trigger when people accidentally drop off and rejoin the call. If you can block out distractions, you can make sure they don't block the flow of ideas.

Ideas aren't bad — but assumptions can be wrong. One of the most common "rules" for a brainstorming meeting is "No idea is a bad idea." But let's be honest: some ideas are terrible. And not addressing the poor ideas during an idea meeting can either lead people to start suggesting wildly off-topic ideas (not necessarily a bad thing) or start shouting down the ideas of others (always a bad thing). And more recent research even suggests that this "no bad ideas" mentality might backfire. In several studies, encouraging participants to push back on ideas and debate options typically yielded a larger quantity of ideas and enhanced the quality of those ideas as well. The trick is to make sure people criticize the assumptions behind the idea, not the idea itself. In other words, debate whether the underlying "facts" of a conclusion are true. So "I don't agree" becomes a more productive "That's an interesting idea, but it sounds like we're assuming _____. Do we know that is true?" Don't debate whether another participant is reaching the wrong conclusion from the same facts. This helps keep the debate focused on ideas and keeps individual participants from feeling judged and shutting down any further ideas.

Leverage silence. If you've ever been in an especially loud brainstorming meeting, you've probably thought to yourself, *There's got to be a better way to do this*. And indeed there is. An increasing amount of research suggests that adding periods of silent generation and silent reflection increases the number of perspectives shared and enhances the overall creativity of the group. Especially in a virtual meeting, only so many voices can be heard at a time — usually just one. And in those situations, overtalkers (and overconfident teammates) tend to dominate the conversation. Adding some time for silent idea generation fixes that. You can either start the meeting with that brief period or encourage people to generate a few ideas before joining the meeting. Even better, encourage them to submit their ideas anonymously, which reduces self-censoring of potential ideas even further, since the fear of judgment is all but removed.

Use breakouts to make a large meeting smaller. The larger an attendee list gets, the quieter each person's voice becomes. When the meeting has more than about six people, you run the risk of losing some ideas entirely. That's what makes leveraging silence so powerful, but it's also a reason to leverage breakout rooms. Most video-calling platforms have a "breakout" feature that allows the meeting's host to assign (or randomize) people to smaller virtual rooms and bring them back after a set period of time. To use these best, make sure you review the meeting's goal and objectives (problem question and constraints for an idea meeting) and then send people into rooms of fewer than four people. Give clear instructions on how long the breakout will last, and also on how to capture ideas from the breakout room and bring them back. Many people use the chat function for this, but I think working collaboratively in a document shared by all breakouts works better. If the conferencing platform you're using doesn't have a breakout function, no problem. Just coordinate ahead of time with breakout hosts who will be in charge of starting their own separate video calls and inviting the others to join them.

Pair and share. Even if your meeting size is smaller, there are still other ways to leverage breakouts. When in the midst of generating ideas, try pairing people up in a breakout room. No need to overthink it; just sort them into virtual breakout rooms and have them start coming up with ideas there. Ask them to share their thoughts with their new partner and keep a list of the ideas generated in the room. When it comes time to bring those paired conversations into the full meeting, don't have them share their own ideas or have one person share the whole list. Instead, ask people to share *their partner's* ideas instead of their own. This has the effect of removing any self-censoring that might happen and ensures that each idea already has at least one other champion behind it. You might even find that the sharer adds to the idea as she's sharing it. "Pair and share" works well whether you're doing a full-on traditional brainstorm or using a different method to generate ideas.

Use ranked-choice voting to eliminate ideas quickly. One of the most common ways to get stuck during the decision meeting is to have people *over*-discuss the strengths and weaknesses of various ideas, only to discover later that only three or four ideas were being considered seriously by anyone. So if the list of possible options is long, consider adding a round of ranked-choice voting to narrow it down. In this method, participants use a written ballot (or online poll) to vote for their first, second, and third choice — assigning more weight to each rank. There will likely be an idea that "wins" this voting round, since it will have the most weight behind it. But that's not actually important at this stage. What is important is that several ideas didn't receive any votes and can easily be taken off the table before discussion resumes.

Applying some or all of these guidelines when facilitating will help the meeting run more smoothly and make the quality and quantity of ideas greater. In addition, they'll help all participants feel more included and make it more likely they'll contribute in the future.

The myth that creative thinking is a solo endeavor gets even easier to believe in a remote setting. But while individuals can generate ideas, the real magic happens when ideas get thrown together and get combined, and offspring ideas are generated. And that only happens in a group. Knowing when to hold the right meeting and how to run it is crucial, and doing so might actually be easier in a remote setting.

RULES FOR REMOTE LEADERS

There's a lot to think about when helping your people think creatively. Here's a quick review of our rules for remote-team leaders:

- Start with a problem meeting.
- Then call an idea meeting.
- End with a decision meeting.
- Open with a warm-up.
- Cameras on, mute off, notifications off.
- Ideas aren't bad — but assumptions can be wrong.
- Leverage silence.
- Use breakouts to make a large meeting smaller.
- Pair and share.
- Use ranked-choice voting to eliminate ideas quickly.

And if you're looking for tools to help solve problems more creatively with your team, you can get several resources, like templates, worksheets, videos, and more, at davidburkus.com/resources.

8

MANAGING PERFORMANCE

Performance management in a remote era means abandoning the idea that presence equals productivity. Instead, smart remote leaders know it's their job to help their team set objectives, track progress, and get the feedback they need to do their best work. It's about supporting your team to do their work, not spying on them to check whether they're working.

For the team at Actionable.co, no task ever seems to deliver the end product that was intended when the work began. While that might seem confusing, it's also the secret to Actionable.co's success as a distributed company. As founder Chris Taylor explained it: "The most important performance tool we have is that we train our team to work out loud." In fact, it was this tool that got Actionable.co off the ground to begin with.

Actionable.co was started by Taylor in 2008 as more of a side project than a business. He had struggled to gain traction early in his career, and in an effort to change that, he committed to reading one famous business book per week and posting a summary and reflection on his website — complete with an experiment where he put the lessons in the book into practice. In essence, Taylor was learning out loud to whomever came across his website. And by the end of the year, tens of thousands of people were coming across his website. They wanted to improve their work and their lives, and Taylor's summaries provided a great way to learn and also take action.

Pretty soon people were asking Taylor to come speak at their meetings or run workshops inside of their companies to help them apply the same lessons Taylor was seen applying online. If it worked for Taylor, and for the thousands of individuals who had improved their performance (and their lives) by taking action instead of just reading books, then surely it would work for work teams and whole companies to try the same approach. That quickly morphed into Taylor creating facilitation kits to help managers run workshops with a single team if they couldn't afford live training. That morphed again, into creating resources for other corporate trainers to offer to various teams to keep learning and applying insights on their team. While Taylor had left his other job to focus on Actionable.co by this time, the workload grew very quickly and he couldn't keep producing everything himself. He needed to recruit a team and build a real company.

When it came time to do so, Taylor decided not to let geography stand in his way. "We've been remote since day one," he recalled. "My general philosophy has always been to find the best talent regardless of where they live and then figure out a way to work with them." As Actionable.co grew, that meant finding more than forty people spread out across half of the globe, with each member working mostly autonomously on projects in short-term sprints before reconvening with the team and deciding on projects for the next sprint.

To manage projects and performance, Actionable.co has put its online calendars to work. The company divides the year up into trimesters. Each trimester is four months long (because that's just simple math), and inside each trimester the team does two six-week-long sprints, with some time for reflection, reconnection, and planning in between. Each team in the company sets an annual target, then a trimester target, and then a list of deliverables for that sprint.

But it's understood that by the end of the sprint, that deliverable likely won't look like what was promised. "Based on what you learned throughout the sprint, your idea of what will actually work will change," Taylor explained. "That's okay. Our focus is on outcome, not activity. We just want to make sure whatever you deliver meets the objective of the project

—even if it looks wildly different than what was originally planned."

Focus on the outcome, not activity.

That sounds great, but wouldn't it be massively confusing if you expected one thing from your teammates and, six weeks later, they delivered something totally different? That's where working out loud comes in. Everyone at Actionable.co is expected to regularly share their progress, promote their wins, and ask for help when they're stuck. Each team holds a weekly stand-up meeting where updates are given, challenges are shared, and progress is tracked. And the company holds a monthly town hall where they review the whole scorecard of where they are in the trimester and what changes have been made. In addition, every two weeks, all teammates meet with the team leader for a coaching call.

Taylor is quick to point out that the coaching call is not a performance review. "I think those are bull," he offered. "Traditional performance reviews stifle the conversation. They become more about presenting progress in a best light — posturing and defending as opposed to discussing and learning. But there does need to be a way to provide feedback to people." So the coaching call becomes the opportunity to review progress and discuss ways to eliminate obstacles to meeting the sprint's objectives. And lastly, everything that gets discussed on the coaching call gets added to a master spreadsheet that tracks the projects for that sprint and the progress (or lack thereof) being made. That way everyone can see where others are in real time and, perhaps most important, everyone can offer help to anyone who is stuck.

For Actionable.co, the system isn't perfect — but it's perfectly tailored to the work that they do. And Taylor and the whole company know that it will change over time. Even performance management is something that will change as they get further along in the process. But Taylor knew that they would have to put a system in place to replace what happens without too much effort on an in-person team.

When you're all in the same space, working out loud often just happens. People walk to each other's workstation to ask questions or chat in the break room about setbacks and progress. Managers often manage "by walking around," which in a best-case scenario means regularly checking in on people, and in a worst-case scenario means spying on people at the office just to make sure they're at their desks and not watching You-Tube.

Sadly, many companies that had to make the quick transition to remote work sought to manage performance by focusing on the wrong thing: they installed software to spy on their employees, just like a worst-case manager at the office. During the COVID-19 response and the resulting work-from-home experiment — sales of monitoring software skyrocketed. Suddenly, every computer at the company was tracking which applications people were using and for how long.

But the spying-software approach is a terrible idea for a number of reasons. For one thing, they're really only measuring whether or not employees are using the right programs — not whether they're using those programs right. In other words, they're measuring activity, not outcomes. Moreover, a significant amount of research suggests that these programs come with several unintended consequences. In a 2017 study, researchers led by Baylor University's John Carlson sought to predict employees' likelihood of quitting their jobs. In particular, they found that companies' use of monitoring software significantly increased employee tension and job dissatisfaction and led to a greater intention to quit. Likewise, a 2019 study from researchers at the University of Jyväskylä, in Finland, found that electronic surveillance of employees did increase their extrinsic motivation (motivation to do the work to gain reward or avoid punishment), but in the long term it dramatically reduced their intrinsic motivation (motivation to do the work because of the joy of working) and possibly their creative thinking ability. Perhaps most important in that study, employees who knew they were being watched were much less likely to put in extra effort to help the company.

Instead of spying software, any performance management plan for a remote team must be built on a foundation of trust and autonomy. You're not there in the office with the team each day (and digitally monitoring them doesn't work), so you have to trust them to figure out how they're going to get done the tasks assigned to them.

And that's a good thing, because for decades now, organizational psychologists have proven that autonomy at work makes workers more motivated, more productive, and more engaged. It started largely in the 1970s, with two researchers, Edward Deci and Richard Ryan, both professors at the University of Rochester. The duo began running experiments to find out what truly motivated humans — a body of work that would eventually become known as self-determination theory. At the core of self-determination theory is autonomy — the ability to self-determine what you work on and how you work on it. This contrasts with many jobs, even knowledge-work jobs, in the modern era, where people are still "micromanaged" by well-meaning leaders who think that dictating tasks and prescribing exactly how to complete them will help employees perform better. "Autonomous motivation involves behaving with a full sense of volition and choice," Deci and Ryan wrote, "whereas controlled motivation involves behaving with the experience of pressure and demand toward specific outcomes that comes from forces perceived to be external to the self." The results of their research favor autonomy in just about every situation.

In one notable study, Deci and Ryan (along with Paul Baard of Fordham University) studied the relationship between autonomy and performance for employees inside major American investment banks. More than five hundred employees were given a packet of questionnaires designed to measure things like how much their bosses considered their point of view, gave useful feedback, and provided them with choice over what to do and how to do it. The researchers also collected performance evaluations for each of the surveyed employees. In comparing the questionnaires and the performance evaluations, the researchers found a significant correlation between employees' perceptions of autonomy and their overall performance. The more managers gave up control over what to do and how to do it, the more likely employees were to do it well.

That bodes well for remote work, since the remoteness wrested a lot of the control out of managers' hands already.

In place of control — or the ability to dictate how an employee is doing a task — autonomy requires remote-team leaders to provide extra feedback and coaching — or the ability to guide autonomous workers toward discoveries that help them improve performance. The strong correlation between feedback and performance was also captured in the Deci-Ryan-Baard study. You won't be able to see your people as they work, but you can give them updates on how they're doing and guide them to finding ways to do it better.

It's also worth noting here that autonomy doesn't necessarily mean complete independence, which Deci and Ryan would be quick to point out. "Autonomy means to act volitionally, with a sense of choice," they write, "whereas independence means to function alone and not rely on others." That again bodes well for remote work — which is often highly autonomous by nature but *also* highly collaborative (meaning more interdependent than independent). So, while some of a manager's control-related tasks might be removed for the sake of autonomy, a new set of collaboration-related tasks emerge.

Taking many of the lessons of self-determination theory together and applying them to a style of working tailor-made for self-determination, the role of managing remote performance starts to take shape. The managers who leverage autonomous motivation need to help their people through three activities:

- Setting objectives (choosing what to work on).
- Tracking progress (measuring how they're doing).
- Giving feedback (helping them do better).

In this chapter, we'll look at all three activities in turn. We'll review the research on how to do each effectively, as well as some tips and best practices from companies where people thrive in their autonomous, remote roles.

Setting Objectives

The first activity that's vital to managing performance on remote teams is setting objectives. In remote work, there's often little to judge people on other than the work they're completing. You can't track the hours worked or the methods used to get work done. And even if you could, there's little evidence that it would be all that helpful. For example, one study, conducted by Erin Reid at Boston University, tracked the hours worked, as well as the output and career trajectory of people who claimed to work eighty-hour weeks versus those who wanted more flexibility for family. What Reid found was that the "ideal workers" were indeed rewarded with glowing performance reviews, bonuses, and promotions, while the "flexible workers" were not. But when she dug into the performance data with an impartial perspective, she found that many of those in the eighty-hour-week group were actually faking it. They were just pretending. And their managers couldn't tell the difference between those who truly worked that many hours and those who knew what their managers were tracking and faked it accordingly.

Don't be the manager who gets faked out. Focus on objectives and outcomes, not how hard someone claims to be working. And while you're setting those objectives, here are a few guidelines to consider:

Set objectives mutually. To increase people's sense of autonomy, it's important that whatever objectives you set, they come out of a conversation about what is needed and what is realistic. You don't want your people to feel like you've just handed them a random set of goals with no consideration of their circumstances or the time frame. If people don't feel a goal is feasible, they exert very little effort toward it. And the best way to make objectives seem achievable is to co-create them during a mutual discussion.

Agree on intent. During that conversation, make sure to communicate the intent behind the objective and the deliverable. As we saw with Actionable.co, often when people dive into a project, they realize that the objective they set isn't actually feasible or optimal, and so the objective needs to change. This is why understanding the intent behind the project is vital. If people understand *why* they're working on a certain project, then they'll be in the best position to pivot the project as needed but still deliver the outcome desired.

Shorten the time frame. I've written in other books about how annual performance reviews don't meaningfully review performance, because the timeline is just too broad to provide real feedback. But it turns out that managing to the annual objectives, or even the quarterly objectives, similarly fails to have a motivating effect. In a study led by Johns Hopkins University professor Meng Zhu, longer deadlines were found to mislead workers into thinking a task was more difficult than it really was. That, in turn, made them more likely to procrastinate and more likely to quit. So keep the deadlines for projects as short as possible. If you need to, break up a larger project into much smaller tasks, with shorter deadlines, to keep people focused.

(This has the added benefit of making sure a project pivot has minimal impact on other members of the team, since they'll see the change faster as well.)

These three guidelines aren't comprehensive, and you'll likely have more to consider depending on the work being done and company policies. But if you hit these three, then you will have set sufficiently clear and compelling goals for the team — and made it far easier to track their progress.

Tracking Progress

Next to setting clear and compelling objectives, tracking progress toward them is one of the most important jobs of a remote-team leader. Taking the time to mark progress toward a goal is a potent way to keep motivation levels high. In fact, research has consistently shown that the most potent factor in our motivation is the feeling of making progress. Harvard Business School professor Teresa Amabile is at the center of that research, and one of her most notable studies sought to capture what Amabile called the "inner work life" or the experience of work. The study followed more than two hundred employees from seven companies over a four-month period. Every individual was sent an end-of-the-day "diary" survey that asked them to reflect on their emotions, moods, motivation, and perceptions of their work environment — as well as the work they did that day. All told, Amabile and her team collected nearly twelve thousand diary entries that ran the gamut from extremely positive to frustratingly negative days.

When they finished combing through each diary entry, the researchers found that — no surprise — employees were far more productive on positively experienced days than on negatively experienced ones. But surprisingly, the most common trigger for what created a good day or a bad day wasn't co-workers or bosses or even giant bonus checks. It was simply the feeling of the individual or team making progress in their work. And the trigger for the most negative days was just the opposite: facing an unexpected setback.

Amabile started calling this the "progress principle." The most potent factor in our experience of work, and hence our motivation, is making progress on meaningful work.

Moreover, as people progress further toward a goal, they exert even more effort toward completing it. Researchers have seen the effect of progress on effort in a variety of contexts — from tasks conducted inside a lab, to fundraisers that raise more money as they get closer to the goal, to my favorite example, people buying coffee at a local café more often when their punch cards get closer to that sweet free cup of joe.

As the team leader, it's your job to create that punch card and demonstrate the progress your people are making in order to keep them motivated. Here's a few best practices to follow when helping track progress:

Check in personally, regularly: Every organization and even every team has different cycles of check-ins they follow. Some start each day with a "daily stand-up" meeting to review progress and update everyone on the team. Others rely on a weekly or monthly meeting. These meetings are great, and the right time frame really depends on the work being done. But none of these meetings should replace one-on-one check-ins that you conduct with each member of your team. You need to be checking in individually at least every other week. Why? Because people may not be completely honest on the team call about obstacles they're facing (and in some cases not honest about the amount of progress they've made — who wants to seem like they're bragging?). So the only way to know for sure where people are is to ask them privately.

Check in with different people differently. These aren't formal performance reviews, and so there isn't any need to keep them standardized among people on the team. Ideally, you're checking in with everyone equally — but equally doesn't mean *the same*. Some people will prefer weekly or even daily check-ins (especially those starting out on the team), while others will feel that interrupts them too often and they'd rather just chat every other week. In addition, how you'll do that check-in might vary. Some people prefer a scheduled video call that lets them discuss a wide range of things, while others on your team will want to send you a quick email with updates and questions. As you get to know each person on your team better, you'll adjust accordingly. But if you don't know, then ask.

Communicate back to the team. Whatever method gets used to check in personally, make sure progress gets captured and communicated back to the team. If you want to develop a system (or an expectation) that your team "works out loud," as in the Actionable.co example, that's ideal. But if not, you'll still need to make sure progress and project pivots get communicated back to the team — especially other members of the team whose work is affected. While you're communicating back, this is also a great time to celebrate the wins one person is making with the rest of the team. When one person on the team is making progress, the whole team moves forward.

But there will be times when you check in with a teammate who is flat-out stuck or moving backwards. And when that happens, your job as a leader becomes one of providing the feedback they need to get moving in the right direction again.

Giving Feedback

An inseparable aspect of managing performance is giving feedback on the performance observed. We've stressed the importance of focusing on outcomes, not actions. But there are times when observable actions are clearly not yielding the desired outcome. In those situations, giving feedback and finding a way to change behavior is crucial. But there's more to giving feedback than just pointing out what's right and wrong — or even putting the two together in that carefully constructed (but awful-tasting) compliment sandwich.

Separate people problems from process problems. The renowned management researcher W. Edwards Deming famously said that "a bad system will beat a good person every time." Or, as Trivinia Barber, of Priority VA (a distributed company that focuses on placing virtual executive assistants with entrepreneurs), put it: "The first thing I try to do when I spot an issue is try to determine if this is a people problem or a process problem." Barber has been at the center of hundreds of remote employee-employer relationships and has found that most problems were actually process problems — instructions weren't clear or resources weren't provided. Taking the time, ahead of time, to determine if the performance issue you've spotted is truly a people problem will save you a lot of time before you discuss it with a teammate and will help you find much better solutions after you discuss it.

Make feedback clear and constructive. Outline specifically what you observed, heard, noticed, or read. Focus on specific, concrete behaviors without assuming any intent behind the action. One of your goals in the conversation should be to discover the intent, but if you state your assumption outright, you'll likely ruin your chances of teammates being honest with you. If you need to, script out your list of actions ahead of time so you'll stay focused in the moment. In addition to outlining what was done, offer constructive feedback by reviewing what should have been done or what actions would have been a better option.

Focus on the impact behind actions. At the same time as you're specific on actions, you don't want to be received as just a micromanager. So you'll need to pair every action with an impact as well. Mention how the action impacted the team or customer or some other stakeholder. Depending on the action, this might be a positive or negative impact. Focusing on impact keeps the conversation from getting too defensive, but it also reminds teammates why the work they do is so important and why doing it well was important enough for you to intervene.

Don't just talk—listen. If you've been a leader for longer than a few minutes, you know that people tend to be happiest and most productive when they feel like they can contribute freely—and that includes contributing to the conversation about their own performance. This isn't just letting them list off "excuses." If you've done the work ahead of time of separating people problems from process ones, then you've already removed that from the conversation. Instead, listening to them means getting a peek into their feelings, emotions, and frustrations as they try to perform. And that will make it much easier to decide on a proper plan of action to improve performance. The best way to know you're listening enough is to track how many questions you're asking, versus how many statements you're making. If you're just talking at them, then you're delivering a monologue — not having a conversation.

Collaborate on a solution. You've successfully brought them into the conversation through listening, and better understood their perspective and emotions. Now it's time to find a solution together. Collaborating on an agreement about future behaviors and actions increases the commitment teammates will make and hence the chances of making change stick. In addition, it leaves teammates feeling like they can come back to you for another honest conversation if something in the plan starts to go wrong.

While we started out discussing feedback in the context of constructive feedback, ideally giving feedback is something done regularly — not only when negative behaviors are observed. If you're checking in regularly, then you have regular opportunities to offer feedback more effectively. Likewise, checking in regularly makes it more likely you'll find those process problems sooner, too.

Managing performance is one of the most vital aspects of leading remote teams, but also one of the most difficult for new remote-team leaders. Without the ability to note when people show up to work, and how long they stay, many managers feel like they can't assess someone's performance. The good news is that those aspects never really captured individual performance anyway. Instead, smart leaders focus on the outcome, not the activity, and make performance management about tracking progress toward those outcomes and removing any barriers to achievement found along the way.

RULES FOR REMOTE LEADERS

There are a lot of moving parts to keep track of when managing performance, especially when doing it through trust and autonomy and not command and control. Here's a quick review of our rules for remote-team leaders:

- Focus on the outcome, not the activity.
- Set objectives mutually.
- Agree on intent.
- Shorten the time frame.
- Check in personally, regularly.
- Check in with different people differently.
- Communicate back to the team.
- Separate people problems from process problems.
- Make feedback clear and constructive.
- Focus on the impact behind actions.
- Don't just talk — listen.
- Collaborate on a solution.

And if you're looking for tools to help implement these rules regarding performance management with your team, you can get several resources, like templates, worksheets, videos, and more, at davidburkus.com/resources.

9

KEEPING ENGAGED

One common misconception about leading remote teams is that it's harder to keep employees engaged. For decades, in-person companies have relied on office perks like free food, foosball tables, or even day care or dry cleaning to keep their people focused and motivated. But in reality, the ability to work remotely often significantly increases employees' focus and motivation. For remote employees, engagement isn't about helping them work harder. It's about making sure they don't work too hard and helping them limit distractions.

F OR MOST OF his career, Mike Desjardins has been working in some capacity to reduce burnout and improve people's experience of work. In fact, it's why he started his remote leadership development company ViRTUS.

"I started this business because I burned out," Desjardins

explained. "Or, more specifically, I blacked out." He was twenty-six and had, by all accounts, a thriving career selling water treatment products. But it was taking its toll. Long hours, lots of travel, and a need to be "always on" to respond to customer requests meant very little time to rest and recharge. In 1998, on a business trip in La Jolla, California, Desjardins woke early to get ready for the day. He got out of bed and promptly blacked out three times. When he figured out what was going on, he called his colleagues to ask them to cancel all of his meetings that day. It took the next three days just to start to feel normal again. It took six more months to process what had happened and actually exit the job that was sucking out all of his energy.

But he made the switch and started ViRTUS to take control of his career and (hopefully) his life. In the early years, the company wasn't remote. The physical office location made it easier to draw boundaries between work and life, and Desjardins was adamant about respecting those boundaries for himself and his team. In fact, they kept growing and consuming more and more office space, moving locations three times in the first nine years. In the summer of 2009, he learned from a fellow entrepreneur about running the whole company remotely and realized what the cost savings and the benefits to everyone on the team could be if they moved to a remote workplace. In the fall of 2009, they took the plunge and went remote. And in 2010, their growth exploded. Within those same few months, they signed leadership development deals with several major corporations throughout Canada — from the largest telecommunications company to one of the largest restaurant chains. The size of these contracts would mean hiring more people, and in the past, that would have meant renting even more office space. It also would have meant traveling all over the country. But since they were already remote, they were set up to grow without having to worry about any of those details.

They still keep a small office in Vancouver — but it mostly just holds projectors, facilitation kits, and other supplies. Desjardins even refers to it as a high-class storage unit. And while becoming a remote company helped make servicing their new clients easier (and saved them a lot of money on rent), it also left the door open for an unexpected old foe to walk back into Desjardins's life: burnout.

But this time it wasn't just Desjardins. It was the whole company. He quickly noticed how working remotely led most of his people to work *harder* each day. Without the physical location providing a boundary between work and life, everyone in the company was subtly tempted into working harder and working longer. "They didn't take breaks. They didn't take lunch. They answered email at all hours of the day," he said. "And suddenly now all of our days were twelve hours long. Within the first six months of going remote, the whole company burnt out."

This time, however, Desjardins was a little more skilled in recognizing the signs — so no one blacked out. The move to remote had threatened his mission to build a burnout-free company, but his past experiences helped him take action quickly. He and some of the other leadership development facilitators on staff turned their attention from their clients to their own company. They interviewed most of the twenty-plus employees on staff and very quickly figured out the problem *and* the solution. They needed to draw better boundaries and provide more realistic expectations and team norms.

The company as a whole took drastic action. They set the expectation that people needed to be responsive during normal business hours in their time zone — and at no other time. That meant they expected their people to be unresponsive at night and on weekends. It also meant training them to put "do not disturb" settings on their phones after hours and marking when they were and weren't at their computers on the company's internal systems.

On top of that, it meant training their clients on reasonable expectations for working with *them* — and for working at their own companies. "I remember when we got serious about boundaries, one of our clients scheduled a meeting during the lunch hour," Desjardins recalled. "This was a company that had just sent tens of thousands of their employees home with cell phones and laptops and told them they were remote. Then they started scheduling conference calls during lunch hours." So Desjardins and his team logged on to the video call with their lunches in front of them. At first, members of the client company were confused, but Desjardins quickly chimed in. "You scheduled the call during lunch, so we brought our lunch," he said. "Why don't you go get your lunch and you eat it, too, while we talk?" Pretty quickly, the client stopped asking for noontime conference calls.

With a different client, the ViRTUS team started noticing that employees in that company were scheduling meetings back-to-back and giving themselves no buffer. So, whenever they scheduled a meeting with the client, they built an agenda that was deliberately fifteen minutes less than the time they had scheduled. They would end every meeting with "Well, we finished the agenda, so I guess you have fifteen minutes back in your calendar." It took a few weeks, but the client started noticing the pattern and asked them about it. "Ultimately, it wasn't about the fifteen minutes. We wanted them to learn to give themselves downtime. And we figured we had to model it first," Desjardins said.

By leading a remote company and working with other remote organizations, Desjardins has been on the front lines of the battle against burnout for most of ViRTUS's twenty-year existence. So he's seen time and again what surprises so many leaders making the transition to remote work. People working from home aren't less productive. You don't have to work any harder to keep them engaged and motivated. In fact, they're often *more* productive and engaged than their in-person counterparts. Engaging your remote team is about making sure they're not working *too* hard. Otherwise, burnout is inevitable.

Engaging is about helping them develop a pattern or discipline that keeps them productive but also healthy.

This discipline also becomes critically important when remote workers face balancing different spheres of their lives, as noted in a recently published study conducted by Dave Cook. The study surveyed sixteen of the most remote of remote workers, what Cook called "digital nomads." These were people who sought out coworking spaces in popular (but low-cost) tourism destinations (mostly in and around Thailand). Cook didn't just create a simple survey. Instead, he built a cohort of sixteen digital nomads and followed them over a four-year period. What he found was that these remote workers struggled in their early weeks of working remotely, because of what he called the "freedom trap." With the ability to do whatever they wanted, whenever they wanted, these roaming workers failed to develop the self-discipline required to be effective at work and to effectively utilize leisure time to recharge. Because they could work anywhere and anytime, they worked everywhere and all of the time, which was fine at first, until they burned out. Fortunately, many of the remote workers he followed eventually did develop that discipline. But the struggle was real (and took time).

When you examine all the research on keeping remote workers engaged, the path to effective remote work involves two wide and deep ditches on either side of the trail — lean too far one way and people risk falling into burnout, but lean too far the other way and people risk too many distractions from a blurred line between work and life. So in this chapter we'll examine the ways remote-team leaders can help their people avoid falling into either ditch. We'll look at the research on both phenomena and offer some practical tactics to avoid burnout and limit distractions.

Oh, and one quick note: These suggestions aren't directed at your team — they are directed at you. If you're sending emails at all hours, your people will think that they should be, too. If you're not making a deliberate effort to limit distractions, then your people aren't going to, either. So model the way first, help them find it second.

Avoiding Burnout

For decades, many in corporate America made jokes about working from home being synonymous with "not working." But those jokes don't reflect the reality experienced by many remote workers. More often than "not working," working remotely leads to overworking and burnout.

In a study of more than seven hundred remote workers across three organizations, researchers Clare Kelliher and Deirdre Anderson of Cranfield University, in England, found that remote workers most often exerted additional effort simply because they worked remotely. The workers surveyed felt that their employer had done them a favor by giving them flexible working conditions (though if you've read this far, you know that it's not exactly a favor to give employees something that helps them perform better anyway). To compensate for this, remote workers intensified their efforts at work. This intensification came in many forms. It could be working longer hours, or shifting hours and doing work tasks during what was supposed to be family time, or even continuing to work when fighting an illness that would have kept them from a traditional office. In any case, the results were the same: workers almost always worked harder than they originally planned for or agreed upon. And working longer hours, with less distinction between work time and downtime, is the equation for burnout.

Fortunately, that equation can be reversed. Like the digital nomads in Cook's study, you just need to develop a few disciplines.

Set "business" hours. These don't need to be normal nine-to-five business hours. But there are very real benefits to working when everyone else is and tackling little else outside of those hours. While technology (and access to work email on your cell phone) threatens to remove that boundary even for traditional office workers, the most productive workers have developed the discipline to bring it back. If you want to stay focused at work and avoid working too much, you need to develop a set schedule for when you're working and when you're not. You've got the flexibility to build large breaks into the schedule — but that's not a reason not to build a schedule and stick to it. With-out these established hours, what's to prevent you from having an idea in the middle of watching a movie and firing up the lap-top to work on it for the next three hours? Instead, do whatever you would normally do to capture the idea so you can return to it when your office "opens" the following day. You might still get pings and notifications outside of your "work hours," but having a set routine will make you more likely to let them pass, and respond next time you are "at work." In the same vein, make sure you know the schedules of everyone else on your team so you can respect their personal business hours as well.

Develop an after-work ritual. Sometimes, in addition to setting established hours, you need to establish a good ritual to signal that it's time to end the day. That could be clearing out your email inbox (good luck with that one) or scheduling times tomorrow for when you're going to tackle outstand-ing tasks. Or it could be a special phrase or affirmation. My friend Cal Newport, a brilliant writer, has a great one. At the end of each workday, he reviews his task list and schedule for the next two weeks to make sure there's a plan for accomplish-ing each task, then he shuts off his computer and utters these magic words: *Schedule shutdown . . . complete.* "Here's my rule," Newport explained. "After I've uttered the magic phrase, if a work-related worry pops to mind, I always answer it with the following thought process: (1) I said the termination phrase. (2) I wouldn't have said this phrase if I hadn't checked over all of my tasks, my calendar, and my weekly plan and decided that everything was captured and I was on top of everything. (3) Therefore, there is no need to worry." That peace of mind is ultimately the point of an after-work ritual — even if it sounds as silly as Newport's mantra.

Change devices when you change modes. In my first real job out of college, I was issued a company laptop. It was sluggish and heavy, and there were always rumors about being "watched" through various nefarious programs. But since I still had my notebook from college, I just kept using it for all my personal tasks. Having to switch devices at the end of the day wasn't a burden; it was a blessing. I still keep that blessing going with mobile devices. I have a smartphone with work-related emails and applications installed and a tablet with just personal social media and entertainment loaded on it. My after-work ritual entails walking upstairs to our charging station and switching devices. I could always go back to work by switching back, but having to walk into another room creates just the right amount of distance to keep me from doing it (most of the time). If you work from your personal computer and don't want a second one, then consider setting up two different users in the operating system. Then just log out of Me@Work and log into Me@NotWork.

Get outside. This applies to when you take breaks or the hours before and after work. Make sure you take the time to get outside and into however much nature is available near your workspace. Research consistently shows that the most restorative break you can take is a nature break, which not only leaves you more restored but feeling happier as well. There's something about getting close to trees, plants, rivers, or any body of water that has a powerful effect on the mind's ability to rest. Taking a walk outside might sound like the opposite of what you want to do when you're tired, but a quick walk through a nearby park or a twenty-minute spin on your mountain bike will leave you feeling much better afterwards than plopping on the couch to watch an episode of *Friends* for the seventh time. In fact, if you still don't believe me, that's okay. One recent study even showed that people routinely underestimated how much happier they'd be after taking a quick walk through any nearby nature. So when you feel your stress level rising, or your energy flagging, don't grab more coffee. Grab a few minutes of fresh air.

Whether you adopt these specific practices into your routine or develop your own, the important thing to remember is that it's about saying when enough is enough and refocusing on other elements of your life. Working from home makes it all too easy for work to become your life. But time away from work makes work better, and sometimes deliberately *not* working is the most productive thing you can do for yourself in the long run.

Limiting Distractions

On the opposite side of the path is a ditch that pulls us toward not working: distractions. It's important to say up front that distractions aren't unique to remote work. In fact, the in-person office is probably a *more* distracting space than a home office or coffee shop (especially if the office layout is open, with long tables instead of desks, and no assigned seating). But every type of workspace comes with unintentional land mines built in to destroy your focus.

It's also worth noting that not all distractions are created equally. Some distractions occur because of the natural derailers that come with remote work (such as family and friends interrupting you). But others might be an indicator that your work isn't sufficiently engaging — or at least that what you're supposed to be working on isn't sufficiently defined. If you're working from home and staring at a pile of vague emails without knowing how to respond, it's awfully easy to have a sudden realization that you need to check social media. (This happens at the office, too — just ask your IT people for a report on how much internet bandwidth is used for Facebook and YouTube every day.)

But there are some things you can do to limit overall distractors and make the temptation to pull away from work for a "quick second" much weaker. And as you've probably already found, that "quick second" is rarely either quick or just a second. Here are a few proven tactics you can try:

Build work/life boundaries. Establishing a few boundaries between work and life will go a long way toward limiting distractions. In the old ways of working, going to work was itself a daily rite of crossing over physical boundaries. The act of leaving home and getting in the car or on a train to go to the office helped transition our minds for the tasks ahead. Now, with the distance between home and work measured in footsteps, not miles, it's harder to establish physical boundaries. But that also makes it even more important. Creating different "zones" in the home where work is done and where it's not can help develop mental boundaries that limit distractions. (This also means changing from your pajamas to your "work pajamas" before you start working.) If it's impossible to build these boundaries within your home, consider joining a coworking space so you can work alone together with dozens of people who need the same physical separation to be disciplined enough to avoid temptations. Before moving into a house with a dedicated office, I held a membership at a local coworking space and would arrive with a fully charged laptop and no charging cable. I had to stay focused, since I had a limited amount of time before my battery was drained. Then I'd go home to charge it up and work on less demanding tasks. There have never been more paid coworking spaces available, but there have also never been more options in terms of various other locations accepting (or even catering to) remote workers. From coffee shops and restaurants to public parks and libraries, there's a myriad of options to go "somewhere else" to get work done if needed.

Build people boundaries. All the physical boundaries in the world won't matter if the people in your life don't respect them. Friends, family, and especially children are likely to consider the days you're working from home as days you're merely at home and hence available to them. If you've set up a regular routine, make it clear that they should consider you occupied during those times — and the requests on your time default to "No." If that sounds harsh, you could adopt the "lunch break" rule — say yes to requests on your time only if they would fit into a regular lunch break in an office job. Grabbing the dry cleaning? Yes. Grabbing the complete week's groceries? No. If you've set up a physical location to work from, make it clear when others are welcome and when they aren't. The single most productive tool in our home is a $2.07 red DO NOT DIS-TURB sign for my office doorknob. It took a little while, but we eventually trained my two boys to respect three visual cues. If my door was open, they were welcome to come in. If it was closed, they should knock first and tell me what they wanted. And if the red sign was on the doorknob, they should turn around and go back upstairs.

Batch your tasks. One of the easiest ways for distractions to creep up on us is when we have very little structure in our day.

You could be working on any number of projects, but somehow you're on Wikipedia learning about Banhado frogs or the Battle of New Orleans. To avoid this, think of your day (or your week) as blocks of time where only certain tasks are done at certain times. This could mean the first ninety minutes of every day is spent on emails and communication, then, after a short nature break, the next ninety minutes is spent focused on larger projects. After lunch is meeting time, both for group meetings and your office hours for other teammates to ask you questions. You could even create "theme days" where the entire focus for that day is one specific project, the next day is reserved for meetings, and the next day is devoted to checking in and giving your people feedback. You might still end up with a few tasks to work on as the time block begins, but at least you've narrowed down your options . . . and surfing Wikipedia isn't one of them.

These tactics may not create an impenetrable wall between you and distraction, but they'll at least slow down the distractors trying to sneak up on you, keep you more focused on work when working, and (hopefully) help you work fewer hours while getting more done.

Keeping your people — and yourself — engaged is a constant priority for any leader. Everyone trips occasionally when walking the narrow path between burnout and distraction. But if you establish some guardrails and encourage your people to do the same, you'll be able to increase the likelihood that they'll stay productive *and* healthy over the journey.

RULES FOR REMOTE LEADERS

There's a lot you can do to help keep your team engaged, but it starts with keeping yourself engaged. Here's a quick review of our rules for remote-team leaders:

- Set "business" hours.
- Develop an after-work ritual.
- Change devices.
- Get outside.
- Build work/life boundaries.
- Build people boundaries.
- Batch your tasks.

And if you're looking for tools to help avoid burnout and eliminate distractions with your team, you can get several resources, like templates, worksheets, videos, and more, at davidburkus.com/resources.

10

SAYING GOODBYE

*Even the best remote teams change over time — teammates
change teams (or companies) and leaders move on. Part of setting
your remote team up for success is helping them say goodbye, not
only so that remaining teammates stay engaged, but also so the
whole team is best prepared for new teams and teammates.*

No ONE SAID goodbye to Laura Gassner Otting on her
last day as CEO of Nonprofit Professionals Advisory
Group (NPAG). But, in fairness, she had spent five years preparing the team for her departure.

Gassner Otting had started the company with a fiery mission
— one in which remote work would play a huge role. She had
had a successful career at one of the most respected nonprofit
executive search firms in the country. But something kept bug-
ging her. "Most retained executive search firms charge one-

third cash compensation for a successful placement," Gassner Otting explained. "That means if I was doing a search for a vice president of a major foundation that paid $300,000, I could get $100,000. But if I was looking for a fundraising director for a local domestic violence shelter, which maybe paid $60,000, I'd get $20,000. But that search is so much harder than the big search. And those nonprofits need our help even more."

Frustrated that the industry had created incentives that didn't align with her values, Gassner Otting struck out on her own to do searches as mission-driven as the clients she sought to help. But that also meant cutting costs wherever she could. And office space was an easy cost to cut. In most of the executive search world, firms sought larger offices in high-value parts of town but very seldom used them for client interactions. "The only thing that happened in the office was that staff got together!" Gassner Otting exclaimed. "If I met with clients, I met at their office, because we want to understand them and their culture. And if I met with potential candidates, I would meet at neutral locations like hotel lobbies or coffee shops — because no executive wants to be seen walking into the offices of a search firm." Gassner Otting couldn't justify paying for an elaborate office. So she didn't. She started working from home, and, as she grew the company and hired more people, she asked them to do the same.

"We got rid of a huge overhead," she reflected. "And it allowed us to actually serve the clients who needed our help the most. We did it by being all remote."

Over the next decade, NPAG grew from just her to a staff of twenty-three people, all working remotely. They built a strong company culture despite being at a distance, and they racked up some big wins — from placements at large, notable foundations to placements at small, mission-driven outfits that they aspired to serve in the first place.

They won so much that Gassner Otting started to get bored. Not bored of the impact, but eager for a different challenge. (Outside of her work, she's also a rower, a marathon runner, an activist, and a parent of teenagers — so you can tell she's driven by the new and ever changing.) Her first desire to move on happened at around the ten-year mark, at which point she started having conversations with her business partner about her intentions and also how prepared her partner felt to lead the firm. Pretty quickly, she realized that preparing her team for her departure would be a challenge. While she was looking forward to new opportunities, it was clear to her that the firm would also benefit from a new type of leadership, but many at the firm needed reassurance that the way it had always been was not the way it should always be. They needed to feel confident in themselves that they could do the work, and do it well, without the founder watching over them. She spent several years just figuring out the plan for her exit, and the last year focused on preparing her partner to become the new CEO and others to move up the chain of command, crafting every aspect of her departure with an eye toward how well these new leaders would do in their roles.

"I swallowed my pride," Gassner Otting recalled. "It wasn't about me and my departure. It was about their promotions. Even in the press release, the fact that I was leaving the firm was buried so far down that we counted on people not noticing." And to some extent, they didn't. It's been years since she moved on to a career in writing and speaking, but she still gets calls from people in her network about whether or not her firm might be hired to do their search.

For Gassner Otting, the fact that no one in her own firm said a word on her last day was the best signal that she had prepared her company for a seamless departure. Of course, everyone eventually reached out to her to say a more formal goodbye. But for the firm, Gassner Otting's last day was the first day of their transition plan — and that's where their focus lay. Just like she'd done for so many small, mission-driven nonprofits, she'd delivered her organization an excellent new leader, one with whom everyone was excited to begin working right away.

Saying goodbye is never easy, even if you're as skilled as Gassner Otting from two decades of helping executives manage the transitional phases of their tenure. So in this chapter we'll cover how to say goodbye in two common scenarios: saying goodbye to a teammate and saying goodbye to the team.

(Oh, and we're assuming both endings are on good terms, in order to end the book on a high note. If you need help firing a remote employee, we've got you covered in the "Additional Questions" section in the back of this book. Hopefully you'll never have to check it!)

Saying Goodbye to a Teammate

When teammates announce that they're leaving, it's always bittersweet. You're happy for them that they've found a new and exciting opportunity — but sad that the opportunity isn't with you and your team. It's also awkward. On an in-person team, there are usually little hints you can pick up on. They're slower to respond to requests. They're dressing nicer than usual, taking lunch breaks at interesting times of the day, and making an awful lot more photocopies than before. After they've given their two weeks' notice, it can still be awkward that you're seeing them from time to time as you work together to wrap up loose ends.

On a remote team, you have far fewer clues. And you get none of those final moments. But that doesn't mean you shouldn't create them. Too often, remote leaders make it all business when employees announce their departure. When I left my remote job to go to graduate school, I gave my two weeks' notice via email (my bad ... but as you'll see, that wasn't the worst move) and received a phone call from my manager about an hour later. Very quickly in the conversation, he started reading from a checklist that felt like a twisted mix of an exit interview and divorce proceedings. When I could tell he was reading, I interjected and asked him to just email me the checklist.

"Oh, we shut off your email thirty-seven minutes ago," he replied.

I felt like I'd been on the receiving end of a virtual security guard and cardboard box. Except that this time, instead of a walk of shame through the office, I was just blocked from talking to any of my now former team, presumably out of fear that I might say something bad to them or to my now former clients.

Instead of treating every departure as a betrayal and a security risk, smart remote leaders know they need to **celebrate departures.** And for a couple of good reasons. The first is that, in a social media age, leaving a job doesn't mean losing touch with the rest of the team. If they've worked together for any significant stretch of time, the odds are that many members of the team are connected via digital channels you don't control (a luxury I didn't have until a few years later, when Facebook was opened to all). The second is that people will be watching the way you treat departing employees. And they'll start to imagine you treating them the same way. To make sure either element doesn't backfire — and because, let's be honest, it's the right thing to do — here's how to respond with grace and celebration when teammates announce they are leaving:

First, **show appreciation and excitement.** Your natural human reaction may be to feel a little betrayed, but try to focus on how much you appreciate their effort and how excited you are for their future. A helpful mindset to adopt is that of a college professor or dean speaking to a graduating senior. All of your teammates will one day be alumni of your company and your team — and wouldn't you rather they reflect fondly on their time spent there and proud of the work they accomplished? This is especially true if you sense that their reason for finding new work was driven by disappointment with this team. Now is not the time to try to "win" in anyone's mind. Instead, it's time to focus on the high points, in hopes of ending the relationship amicably.

Next, **ask how *they* want to handle the announcement.** Unless your legal department is making you, don't lock their email down and tell your team what happened a few days later at the next regularly scheduled meeting. Instead, plan for a graduation ceremony of some sort. You want to create an event in everyone's mind that signifies the end point — and you want to make sure that graduating employees remember that end point fondly. At the same time, everyone has different levels of comfort when it comes to these situations. Don't assume everyone wants a teamwide video chat where everyone brings their own slice of cake. They might prefer to craft and send a simple email to the team. Honor their preference as much as you're able (even if you have to bend a few rules). At the same time, make sure you're finding some way for the rest of the team to also show appreciation and excitement.

Then, **prepare your own comments.** Even though you've known about the departure for longer, once the announcement is made, your team will still be looking at your response and taking their cues from you. So prepare your own thoughts ahead of time. This is a time to again express that appreciation and excitement. It could also be the time to lay out your perspective that departures are less a betrayal and more a thing to celebrate, like a graduation (even if you've only adopted that perspective two paragraphs ago). The one thing you don't want to do is say nothing or look like you have to struggle to find the right words — that will likely end up being interpreted as struggling to say anything nice.

Last, **make a plan for the details.** Your company may already have policies and checklists in place for taking care of logistical issues such as shutting down usernames and passwords and collecting any company property. But make sure you know what that plan is and communicate it — preferably before you make the teamwide announcement, but, if not, then just after. You don't want to end up like another remote manager I know whose disgruntled employee drove his company car eight hours to a Chicago airport, parked it in the economy lot, and boarded a one-way flight back home. All because his manager had only asked him to bring his "laptop and keys" to the exit interview and didn't mention the car, so he decided to make a statement on his way out of the company.

If you're working for a larger organization, these aren't the only steps you'll have to follow. Legal will always have more *i*'s to dot and *t*'s to cross. But these are the steps your team will be watching and that will inform their impression of you as their current manager and how they imagine your relationship will be if they decide to one day move on, too. For many of the same reasons, there are a few things you'll have to plan for when it comes to making your own "graduation announcement" as well.

Saying Goodbye to the Team

Just as members of your team will inevitably move on, you will likely grow out of the position of being their leader at some point. This might be because you've chosen to work elsewhere, or it might be because you've been promoted (or reassigned) to lead a different team. It could even be because your team as a whole has been broken up and reconfigured to tackle a different project. In any of these cases, there are probably a few human elements that were overlooked when legal was writing the procedure manual for "graduating" leaders. Here are a few ways to bring them back:

Prepare your resignation letter. If you're voluntarily moving on to a different company, the first person you'll have to break the news to is your manager. You should still have a conversation with your manager via phone or video call, but that conversation will likely end with a request for something in writing to document. So prepare that letter ahead of time. It should state plainly but politely that you are resigning. In addition, make sure you include your target departure date. The standard is two weeks from the announcement, but it varies by industry. This target end date may change. Your manager may request additional time on the job to help with the transition. Or you might be told that today is your last day. Whatever happens, don't take offense. Choosing a target departure date is less about the ideal date and more about sending the message that your decision is final.

Get right to the conversation. Once you've finished your letter, reach out to have the conversation. If needed, you can schedule the call, but you don't want to drag it out and schedule something for a few days away. It's better to get right to it so that you're seen as being upfront and honest about the news. Since you've drafted your letter, you've already got a template to follow when breaking the news. Even though this is a less formal conversation, you don't need to provide an explanation for why you're leaving if you don't want to. But if you choose to, remember that this is not the time to dredge up old strife, but a time to express gratitude for the opportunities and experiences you had working together.

Get clear on the details. You're now on the flip side of the process we covered above. Which means there are logistical conversations to have about network access, company property, exit-interview scheduling, and a myriad of other possible tasks. Keep a pen and paper nearby during the conversation to make sure everything gets captured. You're moving on to something new — you don't want to keep getting emails from the old company asking for you to mail that laptop back.

Break the news to the team. Ideally on the same day you inform your manager, it's time to break the news to the team. There's no sense delaying the conversation. Even in a remote team, rumors will circulate if you resign on Monday and wait for the all-hands call on Wednesday to announce it to everyone. If you have time and the desire, you might consider reaching out to a few closer members of the team to give them a more personal notice. But whatever you choose, you want to control the narrative around your departure. And that means being proactive. When you're making the announcement, make sure you leave time to show appreciation for everything the team has done for you and recognition for everything you've achieved together.

Bring your manager or the new leader on the call. This is the end of your leadership, but it's likely not the end of the team. If you know who is going to move into the leadership role, then invite that person to join you on the call. Like Gassner Otting did, you want to make it about elevating the new leader, not making a final statement about the old one. If you don't know who the new leader is, then invite your immediate manager to join you. In many cases, company policy might be that your manager facilitates that call. And those supervisors end up checking on the team until a new leader is found. So help your team to know and trust them more.

Explain how you want to stay in touch. In a digital age, this formal goodbye is likely not the last time you'll talk to much of your team. There's a myriad of social networks out there, and you probably have multiple email addresses you use for different purposes. But you don't want people sending messages months later to the inbox you use only for spam or sending you a friend request to the Facebook account that's only for family members to share pictures of their children. So this call is the time to mention your desired method of staying in touch. Give them the email address or specific social network you prefer to use. (And while you're on this step, remember to determine which person internal messages should be forwarded to and include this in your list of checkout tasks if your manager didn't mention it during your one-on-one call.)

Leave time for socialization. This call is your best chance to say goodbye, so make time for the team to say it to you. And leaving a little time for socialization is a good way to leave the team with something other than the awkwardness of formal announcements. You'll likely have a few follow-up conversations with members of your former team. But that might depend on their feelings about this call. If the new leader or your manager is on the call, consider scheduling time for them to chat with the team without you. That person may need to explain what the next steps will look like. But even if not, this call is a chance for the team to process the information together — and maybe even say hello to the new team leader.

Saying goodbye sucks. There's no way around it. It's going to be emotional and at times awkward. Give yourself a little grace after it's all over for how it all went down. You'll likely have forgotten to mention a few things (and you still need to mail that laptop back), but that's okay. Most of us are bad at saying goodbye. But remember that, in our interconnected world, goodbyes are rarely final. They're more like "See you later on LinkedIn or at that conference." But that makes handling the final, formal conversation with grace and respect even *more* important. A successful departure means taking care of what needs specific attention, but also making sure that the prospect of running into each other later is a happy one.

RULES FOR REMOTE LEADERS

There's a lot to think about when it comes to saying goodbye, whether to a teammate or to the whole team. Here's a quick review of our rules for remote-team leaders when saying goodbye:

When saying goodbye to a teammate:

- Show appreciation and excitement.
- Ask how they want to handle the announcement.
- Prepare your own comments.
- Make a plan for the details.

When saying goodbye to the team:

- Prepare your resignation letter.
- Get right to the conversation.
- Get clear on the details.
- Break the news to the team.
- Bring your manager or the new leader on the call.
- Explain how you want to stay in touch.
- Leave time for socialization.

And if you're looking for tools to help implement these rules for saying goodbyes of all kinds, you can get several resources, like templates, worksheets, videos, and more, at davidburkus .com/resources.

Conclusion

Where Do We Go from Here?
Not Back to the Office.

AARON BOLZLE, THE founding executive director of Tulsa Remote — a program funded by the George Kaiser Family Foundation that incentivizes remote workers to find new roots in the city of Tulsa, Oklahoma — has for several years both led and been the lead observer of the changing relationship between employees and employers. "Historically, talent went where the jobs were," he explained of the shift. "And now jobs go where the talent is."

And by all accounts, this shift has been working better than expected.

Tulsa Remote started as a way to test a new development strategy that would diversify the once oil-rich city's economy and strengthen its culture. The idea was simple: Instead of "paying" large corporations in the form of tax breaks for moving to town, why not just pay cash directly to people?

If you're a remote worker and you agree to move to Tulsa for at least one year, the foundation would pay you $10,000 for the first year you live and work in the city. While they weren't the first remote-worker relocation program, Tulsa Remote has quickly become one of the largest community development projects specifically targeting remote workers — and virtually the only one funded by a private foundation instead of tax-payer money.

The initial requirements were minimal: applicants had to be eighteen years old and eligible to work in the state for a com-pany not located in Tulsa. But when the organization received more than ten thousand applications in the first ten weeks after it announced the program — for just a hundred spots in the inaugural cohort — the application process had to be quickly adjusted.

"We wanted to be really intentional about who received an invitation," Bolzle explained. Bolzle himself is a "boomerang" Tulsan who spent time working in New York and San Francisco before moving back to his hometown and seeing how it had grown in his absence. Instead of offering cash to tech workers who sought a lower cost of living, Bolzle and the selection team were focused on finding great people from all walks of life, who do all kinds of work but all want the same thing. "It's about identifying people who are looking for a different quality of life and to make a positive impact on the community they would join." Bolzle and the team did extensive interviews to ascertain who was most willing to make that impact and really join the community.

Of the initial cohort, the majority stayed well past the one-year mark. Around a third of them purchased homes. And even after the novelty wore off, word of the program continues to spread through the larger remote-worker community. Tulsa Remote extended 250 invitations to its second cohort (out of an equally large applicant pool) and now has plans to dramatically expand the size of future cohorts. While the intention of the program is to bring more attention and economic development to an often overlooked city, Bolzle and his team got the closest possible look at (and in some ways even helped lead) the shift from in-person to remote work. He's seen how hundreds of companies in different industries have structured their remote teams, and he's listened to hundreds of individual remote workers share the positives and negatives of the movement.

And he doesn't see that movement slowing down any time soon.

"People got squeezed to a point in major cities that they don't want to be there anymore," he explained. "Historically, we built our lives around our work. But the future of work is building your work around your life — and when you do that, you can pick up and move to any environment you want." And that's not just his opinion; he's seen it in the data. If you think about it, $10,000 is not a lot of money. It basically covers the cost of moving halfway across the country — so the people who are joining the program aren't doing it to maximize their disposable income (even when you factor in cost of living). Instead, they're doing it because they've experienced in-person work in massive office buildings built in massive city centers and found the whole experience wanting. They've had to build the rest of their life around their work for too long and hated it.

They want something else. And Tulsa Remote offers them a chance to try that something else.

Neither Bolzle nor anyone else could have predicted that, barely two years after paying people to experiment with remote work in a new city, much of the world would be forced into a similar remote-work experiment. Companies that resisted the remote-work movement for so long were forced to let up. Leaders who felt it was too cumbersome, or worried too much about lost productivity, were all but forced by a viral pandemic to give it a try. And as the results of the experiment started coming in, they looked as promising as the Tulsa Remote initiative.

Having tried life on remote teams, many people don't want to go back. And company leaders are hard-pressed to find a reason to call them back. The few companies that call everyone back anyway will be in for a surprise when very few want to return. At least not return fully. Many people have gotten the chance to rebuild their lives and have been able to get a healthier perspective on where work fits in their life — which is rarely in the center. And they like that arrangement a lot more.

It's safe to say that the future of the office probably isn't as a place to get work done. (And let's be honest: the office hasn't been a good place to get focused work done for a long time.) In most cases, there will still be offices. But they'll be a lot smaller, with more space for collaboration and meeting and less space for individual cubicles.

As we've seen throughout this book, the added flexibility offered by remote work has not come at the cost of productivity. And even before being forced to try it, the research already supported offering employees the flexibility to work from anywhere. As the 2020 Gallup study showed, the most engaged employees were at the office only one to two days a week. Absences make engagement stronger (as long as it's not total absence). And in many cases, absence makes the company culture stronger. Well-led remote teams can work even better together than teams who are physically together.

Remote work is working. It won't solve every problem leaders and teams face. There will always be more. But we will solve them together. And we'll solve them with the brightest minds from all over the world.

Because we can solve them from anywhere.

Appendix A
Technology for Remote Leaders

Remote work has always relied on technology, from the roads and messengers that kept the Roman Empire connected to the instant-messaging and videoconferencing apps that make it feel like your coworkers are just in the other room. Those tools have never been more accessible or affordable than they are today, but not all are created equal. In this section, we'll look at which technology is the most useful and how to use it effectively. Whether you've just assumed leadership of a remote team or are looking to standardize collaboration, here are the tools you'll need to lead your team.

Project Management

This (*not* your email inbox) will be your home base for team collaboration. The right project management application should have the ability to assign and track tasks, set schedules and timelines, share files, discuss issues, and make decisions. Ideally, this tool should be something accessible on a desktop and mobile device, because different people on your team will have different preferences.

Recommended: Asana, Basecamp, Monday.com, or Trello.

File Collaboration

While most project management tools come with the ability to share files, many don't allow people to actually collaborate on those files — especially in real time. So you may need a tool for keeping company and team files all in one place, where everyone has access to the latest version. That tool should also keep a revision history of those files — accidentally hitting SELECT ALL + DELETE happens more often than most people want to admit.

Recommended: Dropbox, Box, or Google Drive.

Time Management

Time management is key — and it becomes even more important with a dispersed team. You'll want some kind of shared calendar, not just to schedule meetings but also to protect your time and let teammates know when you are unavailable. Many legacy calendars have sharing options, but some of them also let people schedule events on one another's calendars. That's actually a big drawback — who wants to surrender their time to someone else? So the best shared calendars make "invites" the default option, or even invite you to find a time from a set of your teammates' predetermined open hours.

Recommended: Google Calendar paired with Calendly for requesting available times.

Also recommended: Any time zone website you can easily use.

Asynchronous Communication

Ideally, this will be covered by your project management tool. But if your organization is email-dependent, you'll want to make sure your chosen project management tool can interact with email as well. Or — and this would be my preference — train your people to ditch internal email and use the project management tool for all asynchronous communication.

Recommended: Asana, Basecamp, Monday, or Trello. If email is absolutely necessary, then Basecamp is probably your best bet.

Synchronous Communication

Remember: "Asynchronous communication is the rule; synchronous is the exception." So, if you choose a group chat tool, be sure that "always on" doesn't become an unstated expectation of the team. If you need synchronous communication either one-on-one or with the whole team, choose an audio- or video-calling platform. Before you make any choices final, make sure to read chapter 5.

Recommended: Telephones . . . seriously.

Recommended if you're going the "water cooler" route: Slack or Microsoft Teams.

Meeting Virtually

Once you go past one or two people on a call, you should probably move from audio to video. The added visual cues help facilitate the conversation and minimize interruptions. Ideally, choose the same tool for small-group video calls and large all-hands meetings. This tool should also include the ability to host breakout "rooms" so you can have smaller discussions during team meetings or brainstorming sessions without asking people to jump on and off different calls.

Recommended: Zoom.

Ideation or Problem-Solving

Many videoconference applications come with some bare-bones tools for capturing ideas or visualizing what's discussed. You can also always pull up a Google Doc and work together, but there are several better tools out there. Specifically, many of these tools are designed for multiple remote users to capture their ideas, draw out mind maps, or create workflow/process visualizations. Ideally, this is a tool that everyone has access to but that doesn't use up too much bandwidth, so that it can be used alongside an audio or videoconference call.

Recommended: Lucidchart or Bluescape.

Celebrating Wins

It was always easy to gather a crowd and recognize someone for outstanding achievement in the office. In a remote-work world, this might seem a little more difficult. But there are software platforms that let you celebrate individual accomplishments and make it easier for everyone on your team to recognize each other for outstanding work. Some of them even connect to on-line stores or send e-gift cards once an individual teammate has reached a certain threshold of recognition. If your company doesn't have an enterprise license to one of these tools, it might be worth signing up just for your team.

Recommended: Workhuman or Kudos.

Tracking Productivity

Depending on the project management tool you are using, you may need to find a separate tool for tracking productivity. Ideally, this software would also collect employees' feelings about what they are working on and, in so doing, take the "pulse" of your team. This should *not* be a tool that digitally monitors employees or otherwise micromanages them. It should be something that prompts them to reflect on the day's or week's tasks, claim their accomplishments, and signal where they need help.

Recommended: 15Five or iDoneThis.

Blocking Distractions

We've covered the need to protect your people's time from distractions, but not all distractions are the result of overzealous communication. Sometimes it's just hard not to get lost down the internet click hole. Fortunately, there are several software applications and internet browser extensions that let you create a self-imposed firewall between yourself and your most tempting distractions. You can block specific websites, games, or even the entire internet connection for a time period you decide upon so you can stay focused on work that matters. Even if this isn't an issue for you, it's a good idea to try a few of these technologies so you can make recommendations to your team. When distractions are the result of family members or roommates who need reminders to respect the boundary between work and home, send your people a DO NOT DISTURB sign. This will help immensely in setting that boundary with a visual cue.

Recommended: Freedom or SelfControl.

Signing Documents

Sending over an uneditable PDF document and asking others to sign it, scan it, and email it back (or, worse, *fax* it) is an avoidable hassle, thanks to various services that let you manage signing documents electronically while also securely. Some even have a freemium pricing structure if your organization doesn't have an enterprise-level account.

Recommended: DocuSign or HelloSign.

Appendix B

Additional Questions from Remote Leaders

In doing the research for this book, I met with leaders at all levels in remote and distributed companies of all sizes. And since this book was written during the forced work-from-home experiment that was the COVID-19 response, I also spoke with a lot of first-time remote leaders. I couldn't fit all of their questions into the core discussions in this book, so I wanted to take the time now to address some of the most common questions I received (that we haven't covered so far):

How can I celebrate wins without being together in person?

Sure, you can't file everyone into the break room for a store-bought sheet cake. But was that ever really that effective anyway? When it comes time to celebrate wins with your remote team, there are three types of celebrations you should focus on: achievements, milestones, and peer recognition.

Achievement celebrations are the most obvious. When your team accomplishes a big goal or even makes noticeable progress on a little one, it's time to celebrate. Depending on the size of the win, this could be something as small as an email or something as large as dedicating time during the next all-hands meeting to toast the victory. The biggest celebrations should probably be saved for an in-person retreat or an on-site. If you're going to celebrate remotely, it may actually work better to leave it a surprise. Asking everyone to jump on a video call just to eat their own slice of store-bought cake is more than a little awkward. The absolute best remote-team celebrations leverage a lot of surprise, including sending physical awards, food, prizes, or other swag in a box marked DO NOT OPEN UNTIL _____. Then, during the surprise celebration on the next video call, leaders ask everyone to open their boxes together.

Milestone celebrations are often a personal achievement (though company or team milestones like years in business or years together as a team count, too). Effective leaders know (or have systems in place to remember) what these personal milestones are. But they also know their team's personal preferences for celebration. Not everyone wants to receive a round of virtual applause on the next video call. Some might prefer a simple email announcement (and a round of reply-alls with congratulations). Still others might prefer no celebration at all, just a handwritten note from you.

Peer-to-peer celebrations are a little harder to get going but are arguably the most vital way to celebrate wins on a virtual team. In an in-person team, simple high fives or quick words of encouragement happen organically (or at least they do in the right company culture). But on a virtual team, teammates often need a system in place to use for the same purpose. Fortunately, there's no shortage of software applications and plug-ins you can use companywide or just on your team (see appendix A). But whatever app you choose, the most important choice is the choice to use it profusely as the leader, so that others notice and follow suit.

These three types of wins and ways to celebrate are an important part of giving your team the recognition it deserves — and needs. But it's worth mentioning that recognition alone is insufficient. People also need to receive appreciation. And there is a difference. Recognition is the positive feedback you give based on results or performance. It's taking the time to celebrate the win. But it's less powerful when its devoid of appreciation. Appreciation is about acknowledging the value or meaningfulness of those results *and* of the person. It's taking extra time to express gratitude to the person being recognized for how they have impacted you. Recognition is celebrating what we do; appreciation is celebrating who we are. Both are worth celebrating.

What about information security?

Let's be upfront about information security in most companies. If the organization is large enough to have an information technology (IT) department, then you can be sure that they take security *very* seriously. But often they don't take *implementing* security all that seriously. IT will ensure that employees run software only off of the company's own, protected servers. But then they'll hand out laptops to senior executives with little more protection than an alphanumeric password. That's like investing in a state-of-the-art home security system but leaving the front door unlocked.

You absolutely should take security seriously, but remote teams likely pose *less* of a risk than you think. Most major websites, including team collaboration tools, run on secure (indicated by the "s" in "https") servers. That's why you're totally comfortable telling Amazon all your credit card details and exactly how to get to your house. But if you want to make sure your team is totally secure, here's a quick rundown of what to check:

- **Require each team member's computer to be password-protected.** Many personal computers allow users to automatically log in if there's only one user. That's really convenient, until the laptop ends up still plugged in at Terminal B of LaGuardia, but your employee is thirty thousand feet over Omaha.

- **Make sure each team member's computer uses hard drive encryption.** Right now, on Microsoft Windows computers, this feature is called BitLocker, and on Apple's operating system it's called FileVault. Both features change a missing laptop from a companywide panic of password-changing and leak-tracing to a mere inconvenience and small expense. (In most cases, if you require this feature, the operating system will also disable automatic login.)

- **Have your team create auto-generated, long passwords for each website and application you use.** Many operating systems will now keep track of this for you, creating a new and random string of letters to create a login more secure than your old reliable "Password1234." If not, there are several third-party applications that can generate and manage these for you. And while we're talking about passwords, have your team members enable two-factor authentication for the password manager and their work email. Under this system, when you try to log in, the service will send a code to a different device to make sure it's really you. If email or password management security fails, everything else is exposed.

- **Enable smartphones and tablets to be wiped remotely.**

Requiring a password, thumbprint, or quick selfie to un-
lock your phone is pretty standard now, but a surprising
number of people don't enable the "find my" application
on their smartphone, which not only lets you know your
phone is still at the bar in the hotel lobby but also allows
you to delete everything on the phone from wherever
you happen to be.

Information security for remote teams isn't hard, but it does
take a little bit of work on the front end. However, taking these
steps will save you a lot of time in a worst-case scenario.

How can I support the mental health of my remote team?

As we've discussed, working remotely isn't all benefit and no
costs. And one of the big costs is that, for many people, working alone can have a dramatic effect on their emotional health.
And paying attention to the emotional health of individuals
— and the emotional pulse of the team as a whole — helps you
spot burnout, lagging performance, or worse before it becomes
a major problem. It's also crucial to building a supportive, psy-
chologically safe team culture. But it's a lot harder to do remotely. Until they are taken away, we don't realize how much it
means to us to have a friend in another cubicle to commiserate
with. To the extent that you can foster those conversations re-

motely, do so. But know that that won't necessarily cure every-thing.

First and foremost, pay attention to the signs. You are look-ing for deviation from someone's established patterns. Are they sending fewer emails than before? Are they noticeably quieter on team video calls? Are they missing deadlines they normally don't have any trouble hitting? These signs will be different for everyone. In fact, for some, hitting deadlines faster than usual might be a sign that they're *too* invested in work and are headed for burnout (or, worse, are using work as an escape from some other issue in their lives). As your team develops shared expectations and cadence around working together, sudden deviations from that cadence will likely be your first sign that something is off.

When you see those signs, don't hesitate to act. Reach out as quickly as you can. You don't have to lead with "Is everything okay?" You can start with a compliment, small win acknowl-edgement, or other positive message and leverage that into a deeper conversation. You likely won't be able to get them to open up, but you can get them to know that you are there for them should they desire someone to talk to. And sometimes that's all you can do. Other times, depending on the relation-ship, you can be more upfront about what you are seeing and how you are willing to help. A few years back, a friend of mine went public on social media with the fact that he had been battling depression. Within hours, one of his colleagues had reached out and said, "Hey, I'm going to be in your city tomorrow for a few meetings, but I'm open for breakfast, lunch, or dinner. Let's get together and talk." It wasn't until they met for lunch that he revealed to my friend that he'd booked a flight after seeing the post, just so he could claim he would be "in town." But their lunch was the only real reason he had flown in.

In a work context, there will always be limits to how open and honest your people will be with you about their emotional life or mental health. But there's no limit on how available you can be for them should they choose.

How should I handle conflict on my team?

Conflict is unavoidable on any team — at least as long as teams are composed of humans. Just as unavoidable is many people's tendency to avoid intervening when there is conflict and just passively allow tension to build up. On remote teams, this tendency can become even more pronounced. If you're actually seeing each other only twice a year, and synchronously communicating virtually only once a week or so, it's easy to let an offense or disagreement slide a few times. But you're unknowingly allowing wounds to fester. The more people keep their frustrations bottled up, the bigger the explosion will be when it (also unavoidably) occurs.

So don't hesitate. Whether you knew it was part of the job

description or not, you will be called upon at times to be the relationship counselor for people on your team — and during a conflict is the most common time. When you see a conflict arise between two teammates, get them together to discuss it as quickly as possible. Don't try to intervene if conflict arises during a team meeting (it's okay to excuse one member, or both, from the meeting if you have to). But make sure you get both teammates back together to discuss it alone as soon as you can.

During that call, you want to lead both people through a three-stage process. First, give them time to describe the behavior they observed that negatively affected them. This stage isn't the time to assume motives behind those behaviors. Just the behavior itself.

Next, let them describe how that behavior made them feel. Again, this is not assuming or ascribing motives to the other person, but allowing the other person to hear how their actions were received. You can even give them a template for this stage: "When you did _____, I felt _____." Depending on the situation, this could also be where you give each person space to tell the other about the motives behind their own actions.

Sometimes, just these two stages will be enough. Letting each person hear the true feelings of the other and resolve the disconnect between intentions and perceptions is often enough to resolve conflict by itself. It not, then the third and final stage should focus on collaboratively developing a solution for how to behave next time a similar situation presents itself.

When it's over, take a few seconds to document the conversation. No need to be overly formal (especially if the conflict doesn't call for it). A simple email with "Thanks to you both for taking the time to chat today" should be enough. You just want to have a record of the discussion happening and of what new behaviors were agreed upon. Hopefully, you never need to look at this email again. But it's always good to know it's there.

How should we handle salaries when everyone lives all over the world?

When you look at the research, and at best practices among companies who've been remote for a long time, salaries should be leveled and standardized largely without consideration of cost of living. Adjusting salaries based on local rents (or the savvy negotiation skills of a candidate) is a trend that will likely go out of style quickly in an era of more remote and distributed teams. Companies will quickly pivot to paying salaries based on what the work is worth, not what the going rate is where the company's home office or the worker is located. And that's a good thing. (Don't get me wrong: I was the lucky beneficiary of this trend for the first five years of my career, working remotely for a company that paid New York City suburb rates regardless of region. It was great for me . . . but not so great for employees in big cities.)

But adjustments create more problems than they solve. When the talent pool is global, adjusting salaries might even hurt those who choose to live in major cities — why pay more for an equally skilled employee just because she lives in Vancouver? And if you're paying two similarly skilled, similarly tasked employees two dissimilar salaries, you can count on one of them finding out eventually. Instead, standardize salaries based on levels in the organizational chart or a transparent formula that takes into account the position, experience, and skills.

At Basecamp, for example, all salaries are based off the ninetieth percentile of market rates in San Francisco, even though few employees live anywhere near the Bay Area. The company wants to be known for paying well for top talent, but also for letting talent choose where they live and hence what their disposable income will be. It's just that salary negotiations don't happen. "It's hard enough to be good at your job, and then to also be an ace negotiator doesn't seem fair," Basecamp's founder, Jason Fried, explained. More companies will follow Basecamp's lead and find that standardization and transparency actually reduce salary conflicts and discontent among their people, while also giving them *more* autonomy over their job.

What if I have to fire someone?

In chapter 10 we covered how to bring the humanity back to what, for too many, is often a strictly legal process. When it comes to firing someone or having to lay them off, the same rules apply. But now you won't be able to minimize the influence of what human resources or legal requires you to say, so you'll have to work extra hard to emphasize the humanness.

Do it in person or use video. While we made the case in chapter 5 that audio-only communication is better for reading emotions — in this case you'll want to be able to read body language. You'll want to know if the silence on the other end of the line is shock, crying, or something worse. And you'll want them to see the look of concern on your face as well.

Bring a third party. Another reason for video is that you'll want them to see that you've brought a third party — and you *will* want to bring a third party. This will be an emotion-driven conversation, and it can be very useful for someone from human resources or at least another manager to be there to help keep the conversation focused, and to answer any questions you wouldn't be able to. In addition, it's always valuable to have someone else who can verify that the conversation stayed professional.

Lay it all out. You'll want to have all the details figured out ahead of time and in front of you. That includes confirmation that today is their last day, how long they'll have access to company networks, what severance package is available, and what is required of them. If possible, send this list to them as you are giving them the news. Many people's default reaction is to defend themselves and sometimes even try to convince you to change your mind. Having the paperwork done and sent over communicates that the decision is made. It's over.

Offer help, if applicable. If this is a layoff as opposed to a firing, this is also where you'll want to explain what you would be willing to do to help them — whether it's a LinkedIn recommendation or offering to be a reference. Saying what you are willing to do removes any awkwardness they would have about circling back and asking for a recommendation after three months of being unemployed. Offer that help up freely instead. This is also the time to mention any placement services the company offers.

Be available afterwards. Leave time at the end for questions. Because there will be questions. And details to make clear. And next steps to consider. And there may even be a few tears. Plan for it. Don't schedule another meeting right at the end. In fact, don't schedule another meeting for a few more hours, just in case. If all goes well, you'll just have some open time on your calendar. And if it doesn't, you'll be glad you have that open time.

Tell the team. In the chapter on saying goodbye, we covered how to co-script the announcement alongside the departing person. In this case, it's better if you inform the team alone.

Don't go into that conversation without a plan, however. No matter what you say, others will start to imagine it's what you would say if *they* left. So you'll want to make sure you are not at a loss for words that are respectful, appreciative, and kind.

Lastly, **forgive yourself.** It's going to feel awkward. You're going to feel bad. It's never going to feel comfortable. And that's probably a good thing. If the only way to get good at something is practice, then firing is something we all should hope to never get good at. So forgive yourself for not doing it perfectly.

Should I be Facebook friends with my remote employees?

The easiest answer to this question is: It depends. But that is not a very useful answer. We'll try to arrive at a simple and useful answer soon, but there's a lot to unpack.

First, it depends on the company culture and how much it tolerates work-related conversations happening on nonwork channels. Because coworkers who connect on social networks are going to talk about work. In highly regulated industries, where every conversation needs to be captured for potential use later, this is a problem. In less regulated industries (and more transparent companies), this is less of an issue. You also need to get clear on what laws regarding employment conversations exist that affect you and your people. Early on in my career, I remember being on the receiving end of a reprimand email from a supervisor for a conversation I had on social media with coworkers about a work issue. I was the one who had to remind this supervisor that work-related conversations among employees were protected from reprimand by the National Labor Relations Board. I probably shouldn't have posted anything, but knowing the law helped a lot after I did.

Next, everyone has different rules for different social networks. LinkedIn is seen by almost everyone in every industry as the "professional" social network, so connection requests abound. But Facebook is treated by some as equally open and others as completely private. Twitter, Instagram, TikTok, and any social network invented and popularized after this book goes to print are likely even less clear. In light of all this, the best approach is to set your own rules for who to connect with on what network and make those rules clear if asked. Then respect others if their rules differ. (If it helps, my personal rules are that Facebook profiles are for family and close friends, and every other network is a public channel with zero expectation of privacy.)

Finally — and this is an extension of the prior consideration — the team leader probably shouldn't be the one reaching out to teammates for connection on any network. No one wants to feel like their boss is stalking them online. And while that might not be your intent, it's easy for someone with different "rules" for social networks to mistakenly assume it is. In the same vein, if you accepted a connection from one teammate on one network, then you probably need to accept any request from a teammate on that network. Being choosy can easily be seen as playing favorites. (You can always accept and then un-follow their updates.)

Taking all this together, the best simple and useful answer might be:

- Develop rules for each social network.
- Apply them uniformly.
- Wait for connection requests.

After that, be mindful of what you post and what you comment on. If it is work-related, it's probably best to switch to a work channel.

Acknowledgments

This book is the product of a remote team. And while my name is on the cover, I'll confess, I only felt I was "leading" the project some of the time. I'm incredibly grateful to a multitude of remote leaders.

Olivia Bartz, my editor, who had the idea first and, fortunately for me, recruited me. Rick Wolff, my longtime editor at Houghton Mifflin Harcourt, who saw the parallels between Olivia's idea and my past work. And even more members of the team from HMH, including Deb Brody, Ellen Archer, Marissa Page, Lisa Glover, and Will Palmer.

Giles Anderson, my agent, with whom I've worked remotely for almost a decade. Thanks for your spur-of-the-moment email way back in 2012.

Several great minds who assisted me with amazing insights and who helped me — and continue to help me — spread the word about *Leading from Anywhere:* Mitch Joel, Clay Hebert, Joey Coleman, Berit Coleman, Jayson Gaignard, Dorie Clark, Tim Sanders, Tucker Max, and Stuart Crainer.

The amazing remote leaders, some of whom had remote thrust upon them, with amazing stories who made themselves available to me for interviews: Trivinia Barber, Curtis Christopherson, Steven Weaver, Mike Desjardins, Aaron Bolzle, Chris Taylor, Hailley Griffiths, Stephanie Lee, Aaron Street, and Laura Gassner Otting.

The researchers and thinkers who've been studying remote work, virtual teams, and just plain good workplaces since Jack Nilles coined the term "teleworking": Charles Handy, Peter Drucker, Roger Martin, Gary Hamel, Liz Wiseman, Robert Sutton, Herminia Ibarra, Daniel Pink, Amy Edmondson, Adam Grant, Martine Haas, Liz Fosslien, Mollie West Duffy, Mark Mortensen, Barbara Larson, Tsedal Neeley, Nicholas Bloom, Jason Fried, David Heinemeier Hansson, Matt Mullenweg, Bryan Miles, and Nick Morgan.

My wife, Janna, and two boys, Lincoln and Harrison, for respecting the DO NOT DISTURB sign on my office door . . . and putting it on the doorknob themselves half the time, which allowed me to complete this book.

Notes

Introduction: The Rise and Fall —
and Rise — of Remote Teams

page

2 *"working remotely will be the default"*: Hayden Brown (@hydnbrwn), Twitter, May 22, 2020, 9:33 a.m., https://twitter.com/hydnbrwn/status/1263840533144727552.

3 *the year Jack Nilles published*: Jack M. Nilles, *The Telecommunications-Transportation Tradeoff: Options for Tomorrow* (Newark, NJ: John Wiley & Sons, 1976).

4 *"a car or a train seat becomes an office"*: Charles Handy, *The Age of Unreason* (Boston: Harvard Business School Press, 1989), 18; Peter Drucker, ed., *The Ecological Vision: Reflections on the American Condition* (New Brunswick, NJ: Transaction, 2011), 340.

   "one Yahoo!": Kara Swisher, "'Physically Together': Here's the Internal Yahoo No-Work-from-Home Memo for Remote Workers and Maybe More," *AllThingsD*, February 22, 2013, http://allthingsd.com/20130222/physically-together-heres-the-internal-yahoo-no-work-from-home-memo-which-extends-beyond-remote-workers/.

5 *By 2018, only around 3 percent*: Cal Newport, "Why Remote Work Is So

Hard — and How It Can Be Fixed," *New Yorker,* May 26, 2020, https:// www.newyorker.com/culture/annals-of-inquiry/can-remote-work-be -fixed.

A survey conducted by IBM: "IBM Study: COVID-19 Is Significantly Altering U.S. Consumer Behavior and Plans Post-Crisis," IBM News Room, IBM, May 1, 2020, https://newsroom.ibm.com/2020-05-01-IBM -Study-COVID-19-Is-Significantly-Altering-U-S-Consumer-Behavior -and-Plans-Post-Crisis.

Mark Zuckerberg went even further: Kate Conger, "Facebook Starts Planning for Permanent Remote Workers," *New York Times,* May 21, 2020, https://www.nytimes.com/2020/05/21/technology/facebook-remote -work-coronavirus.html.

6   *the company spent more than $1 billion:* Chris O'Brien, "Facebook's West Campus Construction Costs Exceed $1 Billion," *VentureBeat,* May 16, 2018, https://venturebeat.com/2018/05/16/facebooks-west-campus -construction-costs-exceed-1-billion/.

Shopify CEO Tobi Lütke announced: Pim de Morree, "The Remote Revolution: Are We Reaching the Tipping Point?," *Corporate Rebels,* June 18, 2020, https://corporate-rebels.com/the-remote-revolution/.

7   *"The results we saw at Ctrip blew me away":* All Nicholas Bloom quotes are from Nicholas Bloom, "To Raise Productivity, Let More Employees Work from Home," *Harvard Business Review,* January–February 2014, 28–29.

9   *The optimal engagement boost:* Adam Hickman and Jennifer Robison, "Is Working Remotely Effective? Gallup Research Says Yes," Workplace, Gallup, May 21, 2020, https://www.gallup.com/workplace/283985/ working-remotely-effective-gallup-research-says-yes.aspx.

1. Going Remote

13   *"The minute we shut our door":* All quotes from Curtis Christopherson, personal communication, June 26, 2020.

18   *Martine Haas and Mark Mortensen:* Martine Haas and Mark Mortensen, "The Secrets of Great Teamwork," *Harvard Business Review,* June 2016, 70–76.

23 *Studies of superordinate goals show:* Lutfy N. Diab, "Achieving Inter-
    group Cooperation Through Conflict-Produced Superordinate Goals,"
    Psychological Reports 43, no. 3 (December 1978): 735–41.

24 *they choose to redefine their team:* Samuel L. Gaertner et al., "Reducing
    Intergroup Conflict: From Superordinate Goals to Decategorization,
    Recategorization, and Mutual Differentiation," *Group Dynamics: The-
    ory, Research, and Practice* 4, no. 1 (2000): 98–114.

25 *the percentage of engaged employees:* Jim Harter, "Employee Engagement
    on the Rise in the U.S.," News, Gallup, August 25, 2018, https://news
    .gallup.com/poll/241649/employee-engagement-rise.aspx.

2. Building Culture Remotely

32 *"I lied during my interviews":* Joost Minnaar and Pim de Morree, *Corpo-
    rate Rebels: Make Work More Fun* (Eindhoven, Netherlands: Corporate
    Rebels, 2020).

33 *"The time clock means":* Frank Van Massenhove, "Shift or Shrink," Lib-
    erté Living-Lab, posted January 11, 2017, YouTube video, 18:44, https://
    youtu.be/LG4JZDzLmno.

34 *"We provide evidence":* Minnaar and de Morree, *Corporate Rebels.*

36 *"We looked at 180 teams":* Charles Duhigg, *Smarter Faster Better: The
    Secrets of Being Productive in Life and Business* (New York: Random
    House, 2016), 44.
    five elements of a team's culture: Julia Rozovsky, "The Five Keys to
    a Successful Google Team," *re:Work,* November 17, 2015, https://
    rework.withgoogle.com/blog/five-keys-to-a-successful-google
    -team/.

37 *"a team climate characterized by":* Amy Edmondson, "Psychological
    Safety and Learning Behavior in Work Teams," *Administrative Science
    Quarterly* 44, no. 2 (1999): 350–83.

39 *Research on high-trust organizations:* Paul J. Zak, "The Neurosci-
    ence of Trust," *Harvard Business Review,* January–February 2017,
    84–90.

40 *researcher Paul Zak wanted to examine:* Paul J. Zak, "Trust," *Journal of
    Financial Transformation* 7 (2003): 17–24.

41 *"Oxytocin rises when someone trusts you":* Zak, "Trust," p. 23.

42 *survey of more than twenty thousand workers:* Christine Porath, "Half
    of Employees Don't Feel Respected by Their Bosses," *Harvard Business
    Review,* November 19, 2014, https://hbr.org/2014/11/half-of-employees
    -dont-feel-respected-by-their-bosses.

43 *Observing a disrespectful behavior:* Christine Porath, *Mastering Civility:
    A Manifesto for the Workplace* (New York: Grand Central, 2016).

3. Hiring Remote Teammates

49 *The company's main product:* "Deep Look into the WordPress Market
    Share," Kinsta, accessed June 12, 2020, https://kinsta.com/wordpress
    -market-share/.

50 *Automattic now employs:* "All Around the World, Building a New Web,
    and a New Workplace. Join Us!," About Us, Automattic, accessed July
    28, 2020, https://automattic.com/about/.

    employees audition for their role: I interviewed Mullenweg for one of
    my previous books, *Under New Management* (Boston: Houghton Mif-
    flin Harcourt, 2016). Unless otherwise stated, all quotes and facts are
    derived from that interview. Matt Mullenweg, personal communication,
    March 10, 2015.

    "we want the relationship to last": Matt Mullenweg, "The CEO of Au-
    tomattic on Holding 'Auditions' to Build a Strong Team," *Harvard Busi-
    ness Review,* April 2014, 42.

57 *factors that explained the success or failure:* Christoph Riedl and Anita
    Williams Woolley, "Teams vs. Crowds: A Field Test of the Relative Con-
    tribution of Incentives, Member Ability, and Emergent Collaboration to
    Crowd-Based Problem-Solving Performance," *Academy of Management
    Discoveries* 3, no. 4 (2017): 382–403.

61 *Ctrip decided to implement:* Nicholas Bloom, "To Raise Productivity, Let
    More Employees Work from Home," *Harvard Business Review,* January–
    February 2014, 28–29.

68 *"On the first day of work":* Adrian Robert Gostick and Chester Elton,
    The Best Team Wins: The New Science of High Performance (New York:
    Simon & Schuster, 2018), 106.

4. Building Bonds from Afar

72 *"While we wouldn't trade the value"*: Stephanie Lee, "Remote Team Meet-ups: Here's What Works for Us," *Buffer Blog,* January 7, 2019, https://buffer.com/resources/remote-team-meetups/.
    "a North American location, a European location": Matt Mullenweg and Carolyn Kopprasch, "How Buffer Meets Up," *Rework Podcast,* June 4, 2019, https://rework.fm/how-buffer-meets-up/.

74 *loneliness at work has been found*: Vivek Murthy, "Work and the Loneliness Epidemic," *Harvard Business Review,* September 2017, https://hbr.org/cover-story/2017/09/work-and-the-loneliness-epidemic.
    the Gallup organization found: Tom Rath and Jim Harter, "Your Friends and Your Social Well-Being," News, Gallup, February 6, 2020, https://news.gallup.com/businessjournal/127043/friends-social-wellbeing.aspx.
    was found to reduce a person's life span: Julianne Holt-Lunstad, Timothy B. Smith, and J. Bradley Layton, "Social Relationships and Mortality Risk: A Meta-Analytic Review," *PLoS Medicine* 7, no. 7 (2010), https://doi.org/10.1371/journal.pmed.1000316.
    the distant nature of teams: Beth S. Schinoff, Blake E. Ashforth, and Kevin Corley, "Virtually (In)separable: The Centrality of Relational Cadence in the Formation of Virtual Multiplex Relationships," *Academy of Management Journal,* September 17, 2019, https://doi.org/10.5465/amj.2018.0466.

75 *They define cadence between team members*: Beth S. Schinoff, Blake E. Ashford, and Kevin Corley, "How Remote Workers Make Work Friends," *Harvard Business Review,* November 23, 2019, https://hbr.org/2019/11/how-remote-workers-make-work-friends.

76 *their own digital fikas*: Many companies adopted this technique, but the hat tip goes to Becca Van Nederynen and Help Scout for labeling it *fika.* Becca Van Nederynen, "6 Tips to Keeping Your Remote Team Connected," Help Scout, November 8, 2017, https://www.helpscout.com/blog/remote-team-connectivity/.

77 *people who eat socially are happier*: R. I. M. Dunbar, "Breaking Bread:

The Functions of Social Eating," *Adaptive Human Behavior and Physiology* 3, no. 3 (2017): 198–211.

businesspeople who eat communal meals: Kaitlin Woolley and Ayelet Fishbach, "Shared Plates, Shared Minds: Consuming from a Shared Plate Promotes Cooperation," *Psychological Science* 30, no. 4 (2019): 541–52.

78   *Studies show people run faster:* Janina Steinmetz and Ayelet Fishbach, "We Work Harder When We Know Someone's Watching," *Harvard Business Review,* May 18, 2020, https://hbr.org/2020/05/we-work-harder -when-we-know-someones-watching.

5. Communicating Virtually

85   *started as a web design agency:* "About Our Company," Basecamp, accessed June 11, 2020, https://basecamp.com/about.

86   *"library rules" for chitchat:* Katharine Schwab, "More People Are Working Remotely, and It's Transforming Office Design," *Fast Company,* June 27, 2019, https://www.fastcompany.com/90368542/more-people -are-working-remotely-and-its-transforming-office-design.

87   *"it chops your day into tiny bits":* Jason Fried and David Heinemeier Hansson, *Remote: Office Not Required* (New York: Crown, 2013), 13.
"you can not not communicate": "The Basecamp Guide to Internal Communication," Basecamp, accessed June 11, 2020, https://basecamp.com/ guides/how-we-communicate.

89   *In a 2012 study of office workers:* Gloria Mark, Stephen Voida, and Armand Cardello, "A Pace Not Dictated by Electrons," in *Proceedings of the 2012 SIGCHI Annual Conference on Human Factors in Computing Systems,* CHI '12 (New York: ACM, 2012), 555–64, https://doi.org/10 .1145/2207676.2207754.

90   *Asking employees to keep a group chat window:* Credit to the team at Basecamp for this metaphor, which I rephrased and built upon. Jason Fried and David Heinemeier Hansson, *Remote: Office Not Required* (New York: Crown Business, 2013).

92   *a "negativity effect":* Kristin Byron, "Carrying Too Heavy a Load? The Communication and Miscommunication of Emotion by Email," *Acad-*

emy of Management Review 33, no. 2 (2008): 309–27, https://doi.org/10
.5465/amr.2008.31193163.

94 *studies conducted on communication:* Michael W. Kraus, "Voice-Only
Communication Enhances Empathic Accuracy," *American Psychologist*
72, no. 7 (2017): 644.

96 *people definitively preferred seeing the real room:* Noah Zandan and Hal-
lie Lynch, "Dress for the (Remote) Job You Want," *Harvard Business Review,* June 19, 2020, https://hbr.org/2020/06/dress-for-the-remote-job
-you-want.

98 *making room for "small talk":* Jessica R. Methot, Emily Rosado-Solo-
mon, Patrick Downes, and Allison S. Gabriel, "Office Chit-Chat as a
Social Ritual: The Uplifting Yet Distracting Effects of Daily Small Talk at
Work," *Academy of Management Journal,* June 5, 2020, https://doi.org/
10.5465/amj.2018.1474.

6. Running Virtual Meetings

102 *"I've been a remote CEO since 1991":* All quotes and details from Stephen
Wolfram, "What Do I Do All Day? Livestreamed Technology CEOing,"
Writings, Stephen Wolfram, December 11, 2017, https://writings.steph
enwolfram.com/2017/12/what-do-i-do-all-day-livestreamed-technol
ogy-ceoing/.

104 *international survey of more than a thousand employees:* Jennifer L.
Geimer, Desmond J. Leach, Justin A. DeSimone, Steven G. Rogelberg,
and Peter B. Warr, "Meetings at Work: Perceived Effectiveness and
Recommended Improvements," *Journal of Business Research* 68, no. 9
(2015).

105 *a 2019 study from Owl Labs: 2019 State of Remote Work Report* (Somer-
ville, MA: Owl Labs, September 2019), https://www.owllabs.com/state
-of-remote-work/2019.

107 *just having an agenda doesn't enhance:* Steven G. Rogelberg, "How to
Create the Perfect Meeting Agenda," *Harvard Business Review,* February
26, 2020, https://hbr.org/2020/02/how-to-create-the-perfect-meeting
-agenda.

108 *You don't need every meeting to adhere:* Henry M. Robert III et al., *Rob-*

ert's Rules of Order Newly Revised, in Brief, 11th ed. (Philadelphia: Da Capo Press, 2011).

112 *videoconferences mess with our sense of personal space:* Jeremy Bailenson, "Why Zoom Meetings Can Exhaust Us," *Wall Street Journal,* April 3, 2020, https://www.wsj.com/articles/why-zoom-meetings-can-exhaust -us-11585953336.

7. Thinking Creatively

117 *"Okay, Houston, we've had a problem here":* "Apollo 13," NASA, last up-dated January 9, 2018, https://www.nasa.gov/mission_pages/apollo/ missions/apollo13.html.

119 *"Stuff the sock":* Jesus Diaz, "This Is the Actual Hack That Saved the Astronauts of the Apollo XIII," *Gizmodo,* September 4, 2018, https:// gizmodo.com/this-is-the-actual-hack-that-saved-the-astronauts-of-th -1598385593.
before reentering the atmosphere: "Apollo 13," NASA.

120 *"creativity is a team sport":* David Burkus, *The Myths of Creativity: The Truth About How Innovative Companies and People Generate Great Ideas* (San Francisco: Jossey-Bass, 2013).

121 *a classic study in social psychology:* Norman R. F. Maier and L. Rich-ard Hoffman, "Quality of First and Second Solutions in Group Problem Solving," *Journal of Applied Psychology* 44, no. 4 (1960): 278.
a quirk of human behavior to chase consensus: Steven G. Rogelberg, *The Surprising Science of Meetings: How You Can Lead Your Team to Peak Performance* (New York: Oxford University Press, 2018).

122 *when you need to think creatively with your team:* I'm grateful to my friend Tim Sanders here, for developing what he calls a "Dealstorming" method, which I used as a guide for these three meetings. Tim Sanders, *Dealstorming: The Secret Weapon That Can Solve Your Toughest Sales Challenges* (New York: Portfolio, 2016).

123 *constraints actually enhance our creativity:* Patricia D. Stokes, *Creativity from Constraints: The Psychology of Breakthrough* (New York: Springer, 2005).

125 *"What would have to be true for this idea to work?":* I learned this awesome question from Roger Martin. Roger L. Martin, "My Eureka Moment with Strategy," *Harvard Business Review,* July 23, 2014, https://hbr .org/2010/05/the-day-i-discovered-the-most.html.

128 *encouraging participants to push back on ideas:* Charlan J. Nemeth, Bernard Personnaz, Marie Personnaz, and Jack A. Goncalo, "The Liberating Role of Conflict in Group Creativity: A Study in Two Countries," *European Journal of Social Psychology* 34, no. 4 (2004): 365–74.

129 *adding periods of silent generation:* Liana Kreamer and Steven G. Rogelberg, "Break Up Your Big Virtual Meetings," *Harvard Business Review,* April 29, 2020, https://hbr.org/2020/04/break-up-your-big-virtual -meetings.

8. Managing Performance

133 *For the team at Actionable.co:* Full disclosure: I have partnered with Actionable.co to create some of the training content offered on my own website. And, yes, the end result of each project looked very different (and better) than our original intent.

"The most important performance tool we have": All Chris Taylor facts and quotes come from Chris Taylor, personal communication, June 30, 2020.

138 *In a 2017 study:* John R. Carlson et al., "Applying the Job Demands Resources Model to Understand Technology as a Predictor of Turnover Intentions," *Computers in Human Behavior* 77 (2017): 317–25.

researchers at the University of Jyväskylä: H. Jiang, M. Siponen, and A. Tsohou (2019), "A Field Experiment for Understanding the Unintended Impact of Internet Monitoring on Employees: Policy Satisfaction, Organizational Citizenship Behaviour and Work Motivation," in *Proceedings of the 27th European Conference on Information Systems (ECIS),* Stockholm and Uppsala, Sweden, June 2019, Association for Information Systems, https://aisel.aisnet.org/ecis2019_rp/107.

139 *"Autonomous motivation involves behaving":* Edward L. Deci and Rich-

ard M. Ryan, "Facilitating Optimal Motivation and Psychological Well-Being Across Life's Domains," *Canadian Psychology/Psychologie canadienne* 49, no. 1 (2008): 14.

140 *"Autonomy means to act volitionally"*: Deci and Ryan, "Optimal Motivation," 15–16.

142 *people who claimed to work eighty-hour weeks:* Erin Reid, "Embracing, Passing, Revealing, and the Ideal Worker Image: How People Navigate Expected and Experienced Professional Identities," *Organization Science* 26, no. 4 (2015): 997–1017.

143 *In a study led by Johns Hopkins:* Meng Zhu, Rajesh Bagchi, and Stefan J. Hock, "The Mere Deadline Effect: Why More Time Might Sabotage Goal Pursuit," *Journal of Consumer Research* 45, no. 5 (2019): 1068–84.

144 *The study followed more than two hundred:* Teresa M. Amabile and Steven J. Kramer, "The Power of Small Wins," *Harvard Business Review,* May 2011, 70–80.

145 *the "progress principle":* Teresa M. Amabile and Steven J. Kramer, *The Progress Principle: Using Small Wins to Ignite Joy, Engagement, and Creativity at Work* (Boston: Harvard Business Review Press, 2011).

     fundraisers that raise more money: Cynthia E. Cryder, George Loewenstein, and Howard Seltman, "Goal Gradient in Helping Behavior," *Journal of Experimental Social Psychology* 49, no. 6 (2013): 1078–83.

     people buying coffee at a local café: Ran Kivetz, Oleg Urminsky, and Yuhuang Zheng, "The Goal-Gradient Hypothesis Resurrected: Purchase Acceleration, Illusionary Goal Progress, and Customer Retention," *Journal of Marketing Research* 43, no. 1 (2006): 39–58.

148 *"a bad system will beat a good person":* Quote by W. Edwards Deming, n.d., retrieved July 14, 2020, from https://quotes.deming.org/authors/W._Edwards_Deming/quote/10091.

     "a people problem or a process problem": Trivinia Barber, personal communication, July 2, 2020.

9. Keeping Engaged

153 *"I started this business because I burned out":* All Mike Desjardins facts and quotes come from Mike Desjardins, personal communication, June 30, 2020.

158 *as noted in a recently published study:* Dave Cook, "The Freedom Trap: Digital Nomads and the Use of Disciplining Practices to Manage Work/ Leisure Boundaries," *Information Technology and Tourism* (2020): 1–36, https://doi.org/10.1007/s40558-020-00172-4.

159 *more than seven hundred remote workers:* Clare Kelliher and Deirdre Anderson, "Doing More with Less? Flexible Working Practices and the Intensification of Work," *Human Relations* 63, no. 1 (2010): 83–106.

161 Schedule shutdown . . . complete: Cal Newport, "Drastically Reduce Stress with a Work Shutdown Ritual," *Study Hacks,* June 8, 2009, https:// www.calnewport.com/blog/2009/06/08/drastically-reduce-stress-with -a-work-shutdown-ritual/.

163 *the most restorative break you can take:* Kristin M. Finkbeiner, Paul N. Russell, and William S. Helton, "Rest Improves Performance, Nature Improves Happiness: Assessment of Break Periods on the Abbreviated Vigilance Task," *Consciousness and Cognition* 42 (2016): 277–85.
     getting close to trees: J. Barton and Jules Pretty, "What Is the Best Dose of Nature and Green Exercise for Improving Mental Health? A Multi-Study Analysis," *Environmental Science & Technology* 44, no. 10 (May 2010): 3947–55.
     people routinely underestimated: Elizabeth K. Nisbet and John M. Zel-enski, "Underestimating Nearby Nature: Affective Forecasting Errors Obscure the Happy Path to Sustainability," *Psychological Science* 22, no. 9 (2011): 1101–6.

10. Saying Goodbye

171 *No one said goodbye to Laura Gassner Otting:* All Lara Gassner Otting facts and quotes are from Lara Gassner Otting, personal communication, July 2, 2020.

175 *When teammates announce that they're leaving:* I found a lot of different guidance on saying goodbye on virtual teams. Three in particular were quite useful: Teresa Douglas, "How to Say Goodbye When a Remote Worker Leaves," *Medium,* March 18, 2019, https://medium .com/@tdogknits/how-to-say-goodbye-when-a-remote-worker-leaves -37ef2aee01f7; Nick Francis, "Parting Ways with a Remote Team Member," Help Scout, August 8, 2017, https://www.helpscout.com/blog/how

-to-fire-a-remote-employee/; and Kiera Abbamonte, "Bidding Farewell to a Remote Team Member," *Kayako Blog,* December 13, 2017, https://www.kayako.com/blog/employee-offboarding-best-practices/.

176 *need to celebrate departures:* I dedicated an entire chapter to this idea in my book *Under New Management: How Leading Organizations Are Upending Business As Usual* (Boston: Houghton Mifflin Harcourt, 2016).

Conclusion: Where Do We Go from Here? Not Back to the Office.

187 *"talent went where the jobs were":* All Aaron Bolzle facts and quotes are from Aaron Bolzle, personal communication, July 1, 2020.

Index

About the Author

David Burkus is one of the world's leading business thinkers. His forward-thinking ideas and best-selling books are helping leaders and teams do their best work ever.

Burkus is the best-selling author of five books about business and leadership. His books have won multiple awards and have been translated into dozens of languages. His insights on leadership and teamwork have been featured in the *Wall Street Journal, Harvard Business Review, USA Today, Fast Company,* the *Financial Times,* and *Bloomberg Businessweek* and on CNN, the BBC, NPR, and *CBS This Morning*.

Since 2017, Burkus has been ranked as one of the world's top business thought leaders by Thinkers50. He's a sought-after international speaker, and his TED Talk has been viewed more than two million times. He's worked with leaders from organizations across all industries, including Google, Stryker, Fidelity, Viacom, and even the US Naval Academy.

A former business school professor, Burkus holds a master's degree in organizational psychology from the University of Oklahoma and a doctorate in strategic leadership from Regent University.

He lives outside of Tulsa with his wife and their two boys.